Patrick Fennell

Recitations, Epics, Epistles, Lyrics And Poems

Humorous And Pathetic. First Edition

Patrick Fennell

Recitations, Epics, Epistles, Lyrics And Poems
Humorous And Pathetic. First Edition

ISBN/EAN: 9783744705325

Printed in Europe, USA, Canada, Australia, Japan

Cover: Foto ©Thomas Meinert / pixelio.de

More available books at **www.hansebooks.com**

RECITATIONS,

EPICS, EPISTLES,

LYRICS AND POEMS,

HUMOROUS AND PATHETIC.

PUBLISHED BY THE AUTHOR,

PATRICK FENNELL.

(SHANDY MAGUIRE.)

FIRST EDITION.

"I'd rather know the lines I penned
Made one hour pass more cheerily,
More lightly and less wearily,
Than know that readers drearily
Went blubbering on from end to end."
C. G. Halpine.

OSWEGO, N. Y. :
R. J. OLIPHANT, BOOK PRINTER AND STATIONER.
1886.

TO THE

BROTHERHOOD OF LOCOMOTIVE ENGINEERS,

AN ORGANIZATION MUNIFICENT IN CHARITY,

ADHERENT TO PRINCIPLES,

Its Members Faithful to Duty and Unselfish in Peril,

THE CONTENTS OF THE FOLLOWING PAGES

ARE FRATERNALLY DEDICATED,

BY ONE WHO IS

PROUD TO BE OF THEIR NUMBER.

.THE AUTHOR.

PREFACE.

In presenting to the public the following collection of verses—dignified by my friends with the title of poems—I conform to the wishes of many correspondents of mine, scattered over various sections of the country. It is needless for me to say that I claim no merit whatever for them. The major part of them were written to gratify my own whims, as the various subjects would present themselves to me ; and they mirror my mind at the time of their composition.

My object in writing a preface is to explain the tone of several articles, which have appeared in the columns of the *Engineer's Monthly Journal*, to readers who were acquainted with my social position at the time of their publication, and who have yet to learn why I assumed the character I did. In May, 1873, there were several members of the Brotherhood of Locomotive Engineers assembled in the room of Sub-division No. 152, located at Oswego, N. Y., waiting for the time to arrive to commence the proceedings. The *Journals* for April were being distributed, and many complaints were made that the columns were full of letters from engineers' wives. One bachelor in our midst, on the shady side of forty, said he wished he were a Benedict and he would insist on his wife joining the army of con- tributors. After considerable criticism, carried on in a carping mood, I was requested to take the matter up, in behalf of Division 152, and solicit wives for those who were lacking them, so we could add our quota to those who were writing over the signatures of "Wife of an Engineer of Division So and So." I took the hint and wrote the verses headed : " A Member of One-Fifty-Two," and adopted a *nom de plume*. During the time I remained incognito, I not only enjoyed fun myself, but contributed to the enjoyment of all who were in the secret, and many a hearty laugh we had at the numerous enquiries made to know " who is Shandy Maguire?" After about two years the secret was discovered, but not before the *nom de plume* had attained notoriety from Manitoba to the Gulf of Mexico, and from the At- lantic to the Pacific, amongst the railroad fraternity. This I say without the slightest intention of boasting.

If I cannot claim merit for my productions, I certainly can claim that a great many of them were constructed under very novel circumstances ; planned in the cab of a locomotive, many of them written by the flickering light of the gauge-lamp, or at an open furnace door, or when

J   " Stalled in huge snow drifts as high as the stack "

waiting for the shovellers to dig us out, meditated or final words jostled out, passing over rough joints, at a rate of speed of sixty miles an hour.

Those who have read my contributions to the *Engineer's Journal* will find them in the following pages in the order in which they appeared in that valuable publication. They are interspersed with others, in as near the same order in which they were written as a hasty compilation would permit, and the whole are now launched forth to public view " with all their imperfections on their head."

THE AUTHOR.

MEMORIES OF YOUTH.

In a listless mood reclining,
　On the flower-spangled heather,
Where the clover-scented breezes
　Kissed my forehead with their balm,
There a maiden sat beside me,
　Both our hearts entwined together,
As we lingered in the gloaming
　Of that evening's summer calm.

Down the west the sun descended,
　And athwart the sky the streamers
Flashed in glorious golden splendor,
　On that eve of long ago;
There delighted, filled with rapture,
　Like a pair of angel dreamers,
We enjoyed the scene of grandeur,
　And the day-God's parting glow.

Up the east fair Luna floated,
　Through the ambient air serenely,
And the stars began to twinkle
　In the distant dome of night;
With intoxicated rapture
　I beheld my lover queenly,
As her eyes were growing humid
　With such visions of delight.

We were young.   No cloud of sadness
    Dimmed the morning hopes we cherished,
Not a wave swept our horizon
    That could make our hearts despond ;
And our love, as pure and holy
    As ere cloistered virgins' nourished,
Made us happy and contented
    In its idolizing bond.

Ere the moment came for parting
    From our Eden, she consented
To entwine her life's young fancies
    With the boyish hope of mine ;
With embraces chaste and fervid,
    Our betrothal was cemented,
As pressed closely to my bosom
    She did fearlessly recline.

Many years in Time's great ocean
    Have been steadily increasing
Since we drifted from the vista
    Of our early, youthful bloom ;
But the love implanted truly,
    Will exist through life unceasing,
And o'er death will rise triumphant,
    To survive beyond the tomb.

A MEMBER OF "ONE-FIFTY-TWO."

Messrs. Wilson and Greene : I'm an old country
    chap,
From the soles of my boots to my greasy old
    cap ;
I am rough and unlettered, untutored in mind,
Yet, a good-hearted fellow as ever you'll find.
I know ev'ry daughter and son of my mother,
Yet thousands on thousands address me as
    "Brother;"
The reason I'll tell confidential to you :
Because I'm a member of One-Fifty-Two.

So much for myself, now a word for the boys—
The fifty brave fellows each comp'ny employs ;
Officials have boasted no better are found,
To do their whole duty the universe round.
And dear Mr. Wilson, if e're you come o'er
To our beautiful town on Ontario's shore,
Ther's a *cead millie failthe** awaiting for you
From all of the members of One-Fifty-Two.

I notice each month as the *Journal* appears,
Affectionate letters which melt me to tears,
From those interested in all of our lives,
(God bless them, the darlings!) the engineers'
    wives.

---

* A hundred thousand welcomes.

Oh ! lucky "plug-pullers" how bless'd is your lot,
Returning at night to your own little cot,
To see the bright smiles there awaiting on you,
And forty wives wanting in One-Fifty-Two.

Now beautiful readers, a word in your ear,
It comes from a heart that is true and sincere ;
A bachelor's life for myself has no charms,
I'll change for a pair of affectionate arms.
And, faith ! I will love her whoever she'll be
She'll never regret being wedded to me—
Whoever shall wish a good husband to boast,
May drop me a line by return of the post.

I wish a long life to the B. of L. E.,
If true to our motto long lived we shall be ;
In union is strength, if united we stand,
We'll be recognized as a power in the land.
The prayers of the widows and orphans ascend
To Heaven, to bless us, for proving their friend
Reward we'll receive, it awaits us in store,
When brakes are set down on eternity's shore.

A LETTER IN VERSE.

Messrs. Wilson and Greene: 'Tis the urgent
    desire
Of your ardent admirer, named Shandy Maguire,
To be granted a pass in the *Journal*, if so,
I will whistle off brakes, as aboard I do go.
I hope a reward you'll receive for the time
You squander, correcting this doggerel rhyme ;
Then all of my critics may go to the deuce,
I care not a fig for their caustic abuse.

One critic I love—as I wrote in July—
The clear azure depths of a bonnie bright eye,
To send through my soul an affectionate dart,
And soothe with its glances my whimsical heart.
I know of a fair one as bright as the dawn,
With footsteps as light as a wood-nymph or fawn.
She prays for my weal ev'ry morning and night,
And welcomes me home with sincerest delight.

Experience has taught on the railroad of life
The time-card to run by's a virtuous wife.
The grades may be heavy and tedious to climb,
Her precepts are certain to keep us on time.
The curves may be short, the embankments be
    high,
Her prayers for our safety reaches the sky,

They rise from a heart of affectionate love,
To the throne of the Master Mechanic above!

I'll state to the brothers all over the land,
Though young, our Division up bravely can
    stand;
Financially truly, fraternally too,
Are virtues prevailing in One-Fifty-Two.
And now the "salt pointers" just wheel into line,
They fling out the banner of One-Sixty-Nine ;
Success may attend them and guide them aright,
Last star, though not least, of our galaxy bright.

Success to our Brotherhood, flashing on high,
The strongest which floats 'neath Columbia's
    sky ;
It guards us securely with counsels sincere,
And offers protection to each engineer.
Oh! far in the future, sincerely I pray,
Be glory around it as bright as to-day.
Lord answer my prayer is the urgent desire
Of one of its members called—Shandy Maguire.

TO THE LOCAL EDITOR OF THE MORNING HERALD.

(MR. JAMES CRONLEY.)

Dear Jim, since Pete Blair has been captured at
 last,
  And took to his bosom a wife,
Sincerely to make all amends for the past,
  In penance the rest of his life.
Remember, 'tis time that yourself should forsake
  The tricks of the bachelor clan,
By towing some girl right into your wake,
  And steering through life like a man.

Consider how happy your pipe you can smoke,
  As both of you sit by the fire;
How sweetly she'll laugh and ne'er think that
 you joke,
  When swearing she's all you admire!
She'll list to the yarns you'll truthfully spin,
  Of desolate days you have known,
As nobly you steered through the breakers of sin,
  Unloved through this world and alone!

In a few fleeting years, an old hulk you will be,
  Without either rigging or spars;
You will roll in the trough of a bachelor sea,
  The same as all other old tars;

And if married, you'll coast near those spice-
    laden vales,
  Where bright orange blossoms are seen,
With cool zephyrs to sing in your sweet-scented
    sails,
  In Benedict waters serene!

Oh! Jim, think of that!   You are bashful I know,
  And rather inclined to despair;
Up courage! my boy, and a wife-hunting go,
  Indeed, you are as handsome as Blair!
But if you should fail in your cruise for a wife
  Don't ever sit down and repine;
For, sooner than see you run single throuh life,
  Old pard! get instructions from mine!

A REPLY TO SALSIE.

Ah, Salsie, my darling! I've lately been dreaming
  That you are the girl whom I've looked for so
    long;
You stole to my bosom like morning's first
    beaming,
  And won this response to your exquisite song·
I find in that answer you sent to my ditty,
  Of all your admirers you love me the most

I'm sure you are handsome, truehearted, and
    witty,
  Inferred from your lines "by return of the
    post."

Now "Salsie"—that name I will change if no
  · falter
  Will come from yourself, my affectionate 'gal'
Henceforth, till we meet the good priest at the
    altar,
  I'll call you the brief little pet name of "Sal."
"Make haste to the wedding" your motto must
    be, love,
  Long courtships are foolish when states inter-
    vene;
I'm anxious your sweet smiling features to see,
    love,
  I burn from my boots to my greasy caubeen.

But Sal, here's a secret I'll whisper to you, love,
  There is not a dollar of cash in my purse,
I had a few dozen, banks bursted, my true love,
  The time of the panic, I give it my curse.
And both of my eyes are fast fading from weep-
    ing,
  To think I'm as poor as a hungry church
    mouse;
My trouble, dear Sal, whether waking or sleep-
    ing

2

Is—have you some traps till we go "keeping
    house?"

I've a stove, which was used many years by my
    mother,
    A wood burner, Sal, with a fearful exhaust;
Its nozzles I'll open or else it will smother,
    And wood is so dear we must look to the cost.
A bedstead and bed, love, a pail and a ladle;
  . A few earthen dishes, and coffee pot, too;
And, darling! I've also the family cradle,
    As useful to-day as when first it was new.

A heart that loves work, and two hands to
    assist, love,
    Beside what I've mentioned above in detail,
If you have the rest, then I pray don't desist,
    love,
    Until under colors of wedlock we sail.
My brothers all say in our noble Division,
    Considering your wishes for One-Fifty-Two,
They'll vote a donation, make ample provision,
    To testify all their good feelings for you.

And now in conclusion, my true love eternal
    I send to you Sal, beloved of my life,
Soon all my dear brothers can read in the *Journal*
    Another who'll sign herself:—" Engineer's
    wife."

They'll know, after reading, you're really con-
    tented,
  They never need pause your dear name to
    enquire,
For, darling, you'll tell them you never repented
The day you became Mrs. Shandy Maguire.

THE DYING PEASANT.

Old wife, come sit beside me now,
  For I can scarcely see
The sadness stamped upon your brow,
  Nor mingle tears with thee.
The fount is dried, the lids are seared
  From keen and constant pain,
The worst has come, what oft I feared,
  Though seldom did complain.

The moments of my life are brief,
  Its tide is ebbing fast,
And death will quickly bring relief,
  From all my ills at last.
But you will have to linger on,
  Within this vale of woe,
Alone, dear wife, when I am gone,
  For God has willed it so.

I now am bless'd with inward gaze,
　And things long passed I spy;
For death dispels the mental haze,
　Obscuring times gone by.
I now behold the little cot,
　Beside the winding stream,
Where first my eyes beheld you, love,
　Like angels in a dream.

Oh, we were young and happy then,
　And knew not what was care,
Our little world was bounded by
　That valley bright and fair;
The humble church where we were wed,
　Before me seems to glide,
Where to the altar rail I led,
　You, my own blooming bride.

For years I tilled the fruitful sod,
　And all our labors throve,
In thanks we turned our hearts to God,
　And render'd Him our love.
Content and plenty were our share
　Beside the river Nore,
Good health, true friends, and prospects fair,
　Could mortals ask for more?

The sky-lark's song to matins called
  Our dear domestic band,
Each heart, with piety enthrall'd,
  Sang praises pure and grand.
The thrush and linnet told when noon
  Had come within the glade;
The nightingales, in joyous tune,
  Made glad the evening shade.

Thus seasons passed, dear wife, and we
  Ne'er felt the march of time.
Each day we labored faithfully,
  In youth's contented prime.
We garnered in each fruitful crop,
  Our kind Creator sent,
And found no trouble saving up
  Our greedy landlord's rent.

So, wife, the years moved on apace,
  Our efforts seemed to thrive,
And happiness beamed from each face
  Within that cozy hive;
Until the famine years came on
  And scattered death around,
Their baneful touch was laid upon
  The crops within the ground.

Our frugal savings helped to stay
    The wolf without the door;
But constant drain soon stole away
    Our little treasured store.
The heartless tramp of marching men,
    Smote painful on our ears,
They came to drive us from the glen
    That sheltered us for years.

Oh, God! how hard to leave the spot
    We labored in so long,
To see the little vine-clad cot,
    'Wherein we reared our young—
Pulled down to satisfy the greed
    Of him who owned the soil,
Who scorned us in such direful need,
    Unrecompensed our toil.

We gathered close our little band
    And took a last farewell,
Of our afflicted, native land,
    No longer there to dwell.
The tendrils of our hearts which twined
    Around our little home,
Were rudely plucked by hands unkind,
    And we from there did roam.

Beneath Atlantic's restless waves,
  Our tender offspring sleep,
Unmarked the spot, wherein their graves,
  Are 'neath the briny deep.
They roll with many victims more
  Of landlord's cruel work,
All driven from their native shore,
  But never reached New York.

The climate here is hard to bear,
  Though plenty can be found,
By those inured to biting air,
  When wintry days come round.
We always had good friends and true,
  To help us in our need,
They'll prove the same, dear wife, to you,
  When from this earth I'm freed.

Dear Mary, place your hand in mine,
  I'm young and strong once more,
I'll lead you back in youthful prime,
  Beside the sparkling Nore;
We'll hear the linnet's tuneful notes,
  The sky-lark's merry song,
Our Irish birds, whose joyous throats,
  Make music all day long.

Ah! here's our little vine-clad cot,
　Where trellised flowers bloom,
And here's the dear, delightful spot,
　I stood a happy groom.
But where are our three children, dear,
　Who made our lives so gay?
Alas! I cannot find them here;
　Good wife, they're out at play.

They're calling me to join their pranks,
　I'll leave you for awhile,
To sport with them on primrose banks,
　In this our native isle.
A smile upon his features stole,
　His days of life were o'er,
For angels took his sinless soul,
　Where parting is no more.

TO THE MEMBERS OF THE BROTHERHOOD OF LOCOMOTIVE ENGINEERS.

Sobriety stands as our motto the first,
　And ever by us must be cherished;
Remember, dear brothers, intemperance is cursed,
　And thousands, by drinking, have perished.
Touch it not—taste it not—handle not then
　The cause of much sadness and weeping, .
But true to our motto, we'll prove ourselves men,
　And future rewards we'll be reaping.

Sobriety, beautiful gem of my soul!
  While life has a thought worth possessing,
I'll prize thee, and keep thee within my control,
  And give thee my fondest caressing;
I'll shield thee from all that tempestuous crew
  In Alcohol's stormy dominions; .
I'll bear thee aloft through the firmament's blue
  When departing on fetterless pinions.

Dear brothers, a glance will suffice to discern
  The wrecks on life's river now sailing,
Swept on by the tide to that mournful bourne,
  Companioned by weeping and wailing.
So touch not the cup that is garnished with crime,
  The cause of wide-spread desolation;
Although it may beckon with gestures sublime,
  Concealed in its depths there's damnation.

Aloft then our banner we'll wave to the sky,
  And rally around it like true men;
The public pays tribute to those who can die
  When sober, on duty, like you men.
Our Brotherhood, then will survive ev'ry shock,
  Erected on such a foundation,
And stand through the future, its base on that
   rock, ·
  And pointing us on to salvation.

TO THE AUTHOR OF "OLD TAR'S TWISTERS.

(Mr. James Croxley.)

Dear Jim :—My rude, untutor'd quill
   Cuts many a quaint and curious caper, '
Because I seek its aid, to fill
   This ample page of foolscap paper.
Old friend, I've hesitated long
   To tell you truly and sincerely,
In honest lines of simple song,
   I love your "Old Tar's Twisters" dearly.

Those happy, halcyon days of yore,
   When "Jolly Jack," with flying colors,
In every port could jump ashore,
   His pockets lined with scores of dollars.
Alas! they're fading fast away;
   In fact, they've left us altogether,
And only God himself can say,
   If ever more we'll meet fair weather.

Those by-gone-days, when freights were high,
   And owners all wore smiling faces,
When royals proudly swept the sky,
   And shipping-masters would embrace us,
To go with Captain "This" or "That,"
   Who'd sail at noon, or maybe sooner,
Although a meditative rat,
   Would rather starve than join the schooner.

Indeed, those were the happy days—
　　They'll many think we write in fable—
When telling how we'd bend in praise
　　Our knees beneath an owner's table,
To masticate a turkey-roast;
　　No epicure could e'er surpass us,
When stowing tiers of quail on toast,
　　Or "duff" and New Orleans molasses.

We kept the weather-side of care,
　　We also kept ourselves quite jolly;
We clapt a stopper on despair,
　　And took a reef in melancholy.
A boats'n's nip, or maybe two,
　　Would ease all pain and start the chorus;
Then, let the skies be black or blue,
　　We were the boys for work before us!

But times have changed, and so have we,
　　I caught the flood-tide of reform.
You also, Jim, forsook the sea,
　　And in the sanctum braves the storm.
But till life's tide shall cease to flow—
　　Till through the pipe the cable started
To moor us in the watch below—
　　We'll ne'er forget those days departed.

A REPLY TO "MOLLIE BAWN."

"Mollie Bawn," with delight I did lately peruse
The musical lines from your eloquent muse;
I said to myself : " My dear Shandy 'tis wrong
To give no response to that sweet little song ;"
So down in the ink goes my stub of a quill
To tell you that I am a bachelor still;
But you and myself on life's course cannot run,
Because you replied you just "answered for fun."

Besides, my dear Mollie, your notions are queer,
I don't think you'd wed with a poor engineer;
To come to Oswego you say is too far, .
Unless I'd be willing to charter a car.
Ah ! Mollie, my heart is a fountain of love,
And sure as the sunlight is shining above,
If you but consented with me to reside,
A drawing-room coach I'd have sent for my bride.

But, Mollie, be serious, 'tis not your desire
To ever become Mrs. Shandy Maguire ;
Your *nom de plume* hides you securely and clever,
My rollicking brother of throttle and lever.
'Tis truth I am telling—I'll tell somewhat more,
Yourself and myself have met somewhere before.
Am I right, Mollie dear ? "why of course," you'll reply,
And I know you're too cute to be caught in a lie.

Well, "Mollie," a glance retrospective I'll throw,

To that beautiful land where the orange trees
grow;

Where the mocking bird warbles in carols of
love,

To his mate that responds from the branches
above.

Where the sweetest of flowers ne'er cease in
their bloom,

Embalming the air with delicious perfume;

Where the songsters, melodious, awoke me at
dawn,

Perhaps it was *there* we have met, "Mollie
Bawn."

If so, those were days that I fain would recall,

When the chalice of life had no mixture of gall.

Ere the ten-per-cent-off swept the land in dismay,

A cruel reduction of hard earned pay—

Ere the Juggernaut wheels of the panic were
rolled,

To crush us by gamblers, too greedy for gold;

Ere the clouds of oppression cast sadness and
gloom,

O'er the men oft obliged to make duty a tomb.

But the sun of the future, bright hope whispers,
soon,

In splendor will shine, as on midsummer's noon.

No gamblers, "Mollie," can hoard up a ray,
Of the glorious sunlight that brightens our way.
Whoever you are, your advice I'll retain,
And always endeavor to run the right train.
I hope you and I, when life's journey is o'er,
Will be told we're "on time" on eternity's shore.

A WELCOME TO THE " HOUSEHOLD VISITOR."

The H. V. is welcome, thrice welcome once more,
To the homes and the hearts it did visit of yore ;
It comes newly dress'd, and glad tidings does
    bring ;
'Tis as welcome as birds that arrive with the
    Spring.
It announces that trade is reviving once more,
The white wings of commerce now visit our shore;
And last, though not least, the good news it has
    spread,
That dear Doctor Reynolds is living, not dead.

Ah, doctor, I cried till my heart nearly broke,
When I heard you were dead, now I laugh at
    the joke.
I feared I should wander the rest of my life,
All alone, with no hope of becoming your wife.
You know that you swore by the angels above,

No woman but me should be crowned with your
  love;
'Tis leap-year, and now my just rights I shall
  claim—
Come forward and make Mrs. Reynolds my name.

" Petticoat government " now is the cry,
For Woodhull and Spottedtail, banners do fly;
So, come and I'll train you, respond to my call;
Victoria will be elected this Fall.
She'll give you a place through influence of me;
A City Physician no longer you'll be.
Now marry me, doctor, if not I'm afraid,
Your darling will linger and die an old maid.

Dear editor, speak to the doctor, asthore!
And I'll purchase my house-keeping ware at your
  store;
My wall paper, window shades, candies and toys,
For our dear little babies, our girls and our boys,
I am certain you keep the best stock in the town;
Besides you sell cheapest, your prices are down;
There's one thing deficient to bless you in life,
You're just like the doctor—in need of a wife.

A WELCOME TO THE JOURNAL.

Dear Editor : Here is the *Journal* at hand,
    For April, freighted with treasures in store,
From many good writers all.over the land,
    From Mexico's gulf to Ontario's shore ;
From Maine to the far distant Pacific slope
    Contributors many this month can be seen
Expressing contentment, new courage, and hope,
    For the trio who're named Arthur, Ingraham
      and Greene.

Your pardon, dear Sirs, for presuming to write,
    My Muse she insists unattuned I must sing,
The jade is now off in a fanciful flight,
    Although she ne'er tasted the Helicon spring.
The fear of the past for our future's success
    Is lost in the sunbeam of Unity's ray ;
The prayers of the widows and orphans will bless
    The men who preside o'er our Union to-day.

Brother Arthur, the party that bade you "good-
    bye"
    In Syracuse depot, are tried men and true,
And fondly we noted the glance of your eye
    When you said: "At all hazards, my duty
    I'll do."
Abe Shoemaker, Colbourne, Carroll, the three,

Declared every word you expressed you'd
    make good,
With hope in each bosom we parted in glee,
    And soon you were hurried away by "Jim"
    Wood.

Our object is truly enobling, I'm sure,
    Truth, justice, and honor, are links in our chain.
Oh! ills upon ills may those traitors endure,
    Who'd seek to destroy us or cut us in twain.
But if in the course of events, 'twould be found,
    That enemies e're should be met on our track,
Do not yield up an inch of our dearly loved ground,
    Remember the army of boys at your back.

Now Spring has returned to cheer us once more,
    And here is a gem which I found in her train :
"Put the engineer's wages the same as of yore,"
    That means, my dear Sirs, ten-per-cent back
    again.
So, "down in the corner" I'll hie me along,
    And pay every cent to the Brotherhood due ;
Besides, I will sing a short verse of a song,
    Not heard since the panic in One-Fifty-Two.

To Garryowen Mike, ere I close, I will say,
    A *cead millie failthe* awaits you, my boy,
When here you'll visit, all crowned from the fray,

3

Which made you a victor, in railroad employ;
 Be sure your old Baldwin is burnished and bright
  And cheerfully grant every little request
 Of him who the throttle-valve pulls on the right,
  Then soon you'll be sporting a B on your breast.

To climb by gradations is better by far
 Than to step on the deck theoretic'lly wise;
Good practical knowledge is always at par,
 What experience teaches don't ever despise.
Now hurry along to Ontario's shore,
 When you get to Oswego blow brakes and
  enquire,
And soon you'll be shown an hospitable door,
 With one who will greet you called—Shandy
  Maguire.

————

A PRAYER.

Oh, Lord, 'tis seldom that my heart
 Was known to seek thy aid;
But let affliction pour its smart,
 How soon a change is made!
I need no intermediate one
 To supplicate for me,
Prostrated here before Thy throne
 I kneel in prayer to Thee.

The churchmen tell 'tis your desire
  That they should intercede,
To save us from Your dreadful ire—
  It is a selfish creed.
I don't believe such doctrines, Lord,
  For when on earth You came,
You mingled in, with full accord,
  Amongst the blind and lame.

Cathedral spires may grandly rise,
  And bells with joyous peal,
May penetrate the vaulted skies,
  With fervid human zeal ;
But reason taught me long ago
  That from this breast of mine,
My thoughts in penitential flow,
  Can reach Thy throne divine.

You ne'er intended wealth should buy
  Our everlasting weal ;
Yet oft on earth unshrived we lie,
  And pierced by churchmen's steel,
Who barter all your graces here
  With parsimonious greed,
Where we must buy salvation dear,
  Confined in chains to creed.

You gave us air and water free,
　And made the earth to bloom,
For which we left our hearts to thee
　From out sectarian gloom.
Abroad among the fields and flowers
　Thy wondrous ways we trace,
Oh, grant among celestial bowers,
　I may behold thy face.

Now, Lord, my simple prayer attend,
　And guide my wayward life;
Be thou my father and my friend,
　Shield all my days from strife;
And when Your wisdom shall decide
　That I from earth must flee,
Oh, grant I'll ever more reside,
　Dear Lord, in sight of Thee.

IN MEMORIAM—PHILLIP DOYLE.

Dear friend thou wert called in thy youth and
　　thy bloom,
　To go over the mournful bourne;
Many kind friends will lament thee in gloom,
Tears sad and silent we'll shed on thy tomb,
　From whence thou canst never return.

Heaven, thy mercy send down, we implore,
    To comfort each sister and brother;
And send that bereaved one a bountiful store,
Who suffered her share of affliction before—
    His heart-broken, poor, widowed mother.

Though clad in the garments of deep-seated woe,
    Her duty she nobly performed;
She taught his young footsteps the way they
        should go,
Her feelings maternal were thankful to know
    That virtue his pathway adorned.

At parting we murmured in accents sincere,
    For God to protect him from danger;
Then sadly we bade him farewell, with a tear,
And now, to behold him come back on his bier,
    From the far distant land of the stranger.

In that far-away land 'tis consoling to think
    That brother was vieing with brother,
Fraternally bound by a mystical link,
Who'd fain woo him back from eternity's brink,
    To gladden the life of his mother.

But Death to the mark was unerring and true,
    In the noon of his youth he departed;
Yet death had no terrors exposed to the view

For him who from childhood his duty did do
  To her who is now broken-hearted.

Sorrowful tears on his grave we shall strew,
  Forget our dear friend we shall never.
Tho' the vail of the tomb now conceals from our
      view,
All that remain to us mortal of you,
  You'll live in our hearts, Phil, forever.

DECLINING ALDERMANIC HONORS.

Mr. Editor : Grant me a limited space,
  Till I publish a little denial ;
Many boys have me pulled in a very tight place,
  And condemn me without any trial.
Wherever I go they keep poking their fun—
  If you doubt me ask Teddy McCarthy—
They say I must not for an Alderman run
  In our tidal-wave Democrat party.

One very great reason these "kickers" advanced
  Why my nag should be ruled from the race, sir,
"He's a railroader now." For that crime I'd be
      pranced
  'Neath the hoofs of the rest in disgrace, sir.
God help us ! I thought a man toiling for bread,

If he truly and honestly labors,
Could stand up erect, could uncover his head,
And be peer to his proudest of neighbors!

Should I measure my strength with opponents,
    I'm sure,
  When the votes in the box would be tallied,
That an Alderman's chair I could sit in secure,
  That the boys of the ward round me rallied.
By remaining away I'll have frolic galore!
  And I hope you'll not think me uncivil
By saying: "I don't care where runs the Lake
    Shore,
  And the Ellen Street bridge to the devil!"

Considering the number of nags on the track,
  'Tis hard to tell which one will answer;
For each is a played-out, political hack,
  And an old, spavined, blustering prancer.
Down amongst the spectators I'm going to stand,
  It is there I'll feel jovial and hearty;
And the nag that's in first I will pat with my hand,
  On the Bloomingdale road of the party.

Mr. Page, 'tis to you I would briefly suggest,
  In my broadest of broad nomenclature,
And I hope you'll bring forward this little request

Up before our New York legislature:
"All the blocks of the Fifth into wards must be
    made."
Or, if not, the whole city will scoff us,
We all hanker so much for the Alderman's trade,
And one-tenth of us then may get office.

TO ANGELINE S.

Miss Angeline S., don't you think it is time
To send a response to your sweet little rhyme?
It thrilled me, it filled me with pleasure all o'er,
I cherished it up in my heart's dearest core,
To think that a lady possessed of your charms
Will fold me for life in your beautiful arms,
And make me the paramount lord of your purse
When once we're united for better or worse.

Lamenting in sorrow, long years I delayed,
Too bashful to woo, and to win a fair maid,
Deficient in courage, both luckless and poor,
What maid such a fool of a man could endure?
But you, like an angel sent down from above,
Spread o'er me the wings of affection and love,
And made my heart buoyant and light as a
    feather
To know we will jog on life's railroad together.

What is beauty? I care not a fig, my dear girl,
If your head could'nt boast of a ringlet or curl;
If your eyes stood at angles of ninety degrees;
If your tongue was incessantly running to tease;
If your nose was a pug, with the top of it red;
If your sweet little mouth semi-circled your head;
In fact, I don't care how your features appear,
So long as a carriage you ride in, my dear.

I hope my appearance won't give you much care;
Of beauty I have but a miserly share;
I'm an only son, in her moments of joy,
My mother oft called me "her handsomest boy."
She suffered with fear least her darling would
    smother,
By ladies embracing the son of my mother.
I wish the dear creatures would take my advice,
And continue, its naughty, folks say, but its nice.

I'm off for Fort Wayne when I draw my next pay,
I'll visit some friends whom I know on the way.
Be sure in your coach to the station you'll ride
To meet me, and give me a seat at your side.
I feel as if fortune, so hard in the past,
Was turning around in my favor at last.
No longer I'll suffer the pangs of distress,
When spending your ducats, Miss Angeline S.

TO W. B. PHELPS.

(On being presented with a set of beautiful razors.)

How oft with microscopic glance
   In mid-teens I my chin did scan,
In search of stunted down's advance,
   Which would denote the future man.
And when a stray, forlorn hair
Did bless my persevering stare,
The razor of my sire I stole;
In boyish glee beyond control
I sought an unfrequented place,
My trembling hand went o'er my face,
No mirror back my visage gave,
It was my first, my maiden shave;
Your retrospective glance may tell
By like experience what befell;
If eight old cats, I truly swear,
   Played hide and seek round each jawbone,
Or danced a modern lanciers there,
   Their claws would have more mercy shown.

And next in years of riper growth,
   Till yesterday at manhood's noon,
I must confess to many an oath
   I stilled, sir, at features hewn.
I slashed, and scraped, and strapped, and
   moaned,

I lathered, rubbed, I tugged, and honed;
The thousand angry tears I shed,
The million crimson drops I bled,
If 1 could but recall them here,
   And give them tongues to sound your
     praise,
They'd thank you, sir, with words sincere,
   In volumes of immortal lays!

Your princely gifts I well may prize
   As souvenirs till life's decline;
They will remind my gloating eyes
   Of many a kindly act of thine.
Their polished, tempered, faultless sheen
Glides o'er my features, smooth and keen;
'Tis pleasure now where all was pain;
And ere I close this simple strain
Of Heaven one little gift I crave
To grant me here this side the grave—
'Tis this: O Lord, if vandal boor
   Should steal, 'twixt now and days remote,
My beauties bright, send vengeance sure,
And make them cut his thievish throat.

TO MIKE OF GARRYOWEN.

Friend Michael : I have a spare moment or two,
And cheerfully now I'll devote them to you.
My memory points me a beautiful glade,
'Tis canopied o'er by an evergreen shade ;
There I'll convey you, my brother in rhyme,
The strings of my harp into tune I will chime,
I'll sing you a brief little sketch of my life
And the luck I have met advertising a wife.

In youth I was orphaned ; no kindred came near
To soothe me in sorrow or stay the sad tear,
When grown up to manhood I thought of a wife
To help me to climb up the grades of this life ;
Some dear little maiden, a sly little elf,
With no other failing than loving myself ;
To lift from my shoulders toil's wearisome load,
When home I'd return from a day on the road.

That's why in the *Journal* I fished for a mate.
A bouncing grass-widow kept nibbling the bait.
She wrote me : "Dear Shandy, in sadness I mourn
"The absence of one who is slow to return.
"But why should I longer lament him in tears ?
"Come wed me and father my two little dears."
I'd like to comply, but my mother of yore
Cried : Shandy, beware of grass-widows, asthore !

Success on occasions seemed hovering nigh,
My heart then dilated with hope-beaming joy,
When "Salsie" with promises sweetly expressed,
Averred she adored me the dearest and best.
I flew to the garret on pinions of love
In search of my bedding, chairs, cradle and stove.
Some friends at our wedding I then did invite,
But "Salsie" soon ended my dream of delight.

"Mollie Bawn" was the next urged me on to
    revealing
A kind of a, sort of a Benedict feeling.
I made all arrangements to speedily wed her;
The rest of my life I would run double-header.
Ah! surely, I thought, 'tis a glorious selection,
This fair one must be the full type of perfection.
Alas! I discovered the greatest of folly
In trying to capture a maiden like "Mollie."

Now last, though not least, well, in fact what I'd
    call
My heartless deceiver—Queen Bee of them all.
Miss Angeline S. left me stricken with pain;
She's possessed of a fortune and lives in Fort
    Wayne.
To the hill-top of hope on love's wings did I go,
But the fickle jade's silence soon dashed me below.

Dear Michael, her reasons are easily seen,
She rides in a carriage, I on a McQueen.

But why should your humble admirer despair,
Whose negligent curls have not a gray hair?
While life lasts, there's hope, and if luck's at my
    side,
Surely sooner or later I'll capture a bride.
But Michael, there's one at my elbow who says :
"All bigamists pay for their amorous ways."
So, between you and I, the state prison I'll shun,
Though the brothers insist I must keep up the fun.

    *   *   *   *   *   *

I see you are one of that brave-hearted band,
Whom a traitor has scattered all over the land.
'Tis better to be found on the side that is right,
Than to pander and kneel to oppression and
    might;
'Tis better to be poor and be hopeful in God,
Than to bow down and kiss a tyrannical rod ;
'Tis better in rags to plod on to the grave,
Than to meekly submit to be scourged as a slave.

But why should I longer this subject pursue?
'Tis gone to oblivion, away from our view ;
If further I'd chime on such dissonant strings,
Brothers Arthur and Greene would be clipping
    my wings.

Right here at Oswego they paid us a call,
And departed with hearty good wishes for all.
My regards to you, Mike, till existence doth end
I shall always be proud to be classed as your
    friend.

"PATIENCE."

'Tis easy to preach about patience,
    For those who have freedom from ills,
When dealing out sympathy freely,
    To victims of fevers and chills ;
'Tis easy to preach about patience
    For those who have naught but a sneer
To give to the wretch who is tortured
    With pains at the butt of his ear.

How eloquent, fluent, and freely
    Their tide of glib sayings roll out,
To soothe the poor victim when howling
    With terrible twists of the gout ;
Or joints all aflame with rheumatics,
    When up from the bed he will leap,
To hear them exclaim : "Now be patient,
    Lie still and go gently to sleep."

With pains of neuralgia thumping
    Your nerves with big sledge-hammer blows,

Or chronic catarrh persecuting
   Your features, distorting your nose.
'Tis easy to preach about patience
   For those with demoniac grins,
Who tell you such torture was given
   As certain atonement for sins.

Some toothaches most surely will bother
   The wisest in surgical lore,
No matter how gently their forceps
   Will touch you, in pain you will roar;
And yet some old midwife or other
   Will laugh at the nerve you display,
When wrenched till your eyeballs are start-
     ing
   From blood-colored sockets away.

Be patient the preachers keep telling
   Poor souls without clothing or food,
When rolling in richest of broadcloth,
   And aping a sanctified mood.
They'll feed you on texts from the Scriptures,
   And ask why you dare to complain,
While at the same time they're regaling
   On porter-house steak and champagne.

Oh, out on such hypocrite swaddlers,
   Who travel palavering round,

To deal out their stock of set phrases
   Where ever affliction is found.
I'd rather have one touch magnetic
   In kindness steal over my head,
Than all of their blatherskite blabbing,
   Dealt out at the side of my bed.

A TRIP IN CHARON'S FERRY.

One night, to enjoy a few hours of repose,
I coiled myself up in the bed 'neath the clothes,
Oblivious alike of my friends or my foes,
   Right soon I was off in a dream.
I dreamt that old Charon had ferried me o'er,
As soon as his boat touched the Stygian shore,
"Here's Shandy Maguire," the old rascal did roar
   With a weird and unearthly scream!

Indeed, 'twas a burning reception I got,
The atmosphere there was oppressively hot,
But the imps whom I saw seemed content with
   their lot,
   And said I would soon be the same.
Old Pluto came up and extended his hand,
He spoke in a voice I could well understand,
"Dear Mr. Maguire, I'm at your command,
   Your wish you have only to name."
     4

To see how his majesty relished a joke,
I asked for a pipe and tobacco to smoke,
That simple request was a masterly stroke,
    His countenance beamed with a grin.
"Here by my side sit at ease and enjoy
A smoke from my pipe, you're a broth of a boy,
While with me you linger none shall you annoy,
    You seldom were guilty of sin."

His devils he ordered to march in review,
Oh, many were there in my life-time I knew!
Jovial companions I saw 'mongst them too,
    And bachelors mostly I spied!
"How is it I don't see a Benedict here?"
Pluto replied with a wink and a leer—
"Poor souls, they all soar to a happier sphere!
    • They atoned for their sins ere they died."

My brothers were few, as the column passed by,
The good natured phiz of "Square" Blake I could
    spy,
He gave me a glance from his amorous eye,
    And asked for the news from above.
I answered: "your sweet-hearts I tried to console,
Alas! surely their grief was beyond my control;
Together we prayed for repose of your soul."
    Quoth Bill, "that was brotherly love,"

Railroad directors were there in galore,
Presidents also, a plentiful store,
Superintendents I saw by the score,
  Beelzebub caught them at last.
There they were shackled both safe and secure,
Placarded "tyrants on earth to the poor,"
Those "ten-per-cent-off" boys I could'nt endure
  I closed my eyes till they had passed.

I also discerned some traitors were there,
A sorrowful, heart-rending look of despair
All of the double-dyed villians did wear,
  My pity for those was sincere.
"Your majesty," then I began, "I would fain
Have you ease the poor wretches of part of their
  pain ;"
From a good hearty laugh Pluto could'nt refrain,
  He whispered "last Fall" * in my ear.

A rollicking, frolicking, musical throng,
Uproariously singing a comical song
Up close to the traitors came marching along ;
  "Who are they, your majesty, pray ?"
"Why, Shandy, a few of the boys I enrolled,

---

* This allusion has reference to the strikes in the Fall of '73, when the Brotherhood was supposed to have been betrayed by Chas. Wilson, the Grand Chief. In support of the supposition, there was a special convention called to convene at Cleveland in February, 1874, and by a unanimous vote he was deposed. P. M. Arthur, the present Grand Chief, was elected in his stead. Mr. Arthur is an intelligent, christian gentleman, and has the entire confidence of the organization, which he has successfully controlled for the past eleven years.

To see that the traitors don't suffer with cold;
They could'nt be bribed with position or gold—
     Here "every dog has his day."

His majesty's pipe I returned and said—
"There's many an honest man toiling for bread,
Who'll better his fortune when once he is dead."
     I tickled the Governor there.
"If this is the region of brimstone and fire,
You'll find a good subject in Shandy Maguire."
After my wants he began to inquire,
     And spoke to me candid and fair.

"Dear Shandy, you always worked bravely on
    earth;
You've earned your grub from the moment of
    birth,
You seasoned it, too, with a sprinkling of mirth,
     And never bowed down to despair.
Receive your reward—you're possessed of the
    knack
To oversee imps I have ballasting track;
I'm building a road up to Wall street and back,
     To handle the traffic from there.

Here comes your gang, they were all millionaires
Above, and were known as the Bulls and Bears,
They gambled in stocks and they cornered the
    shares

Now take all of them you can find.
Oh, yes, Mr. Pluto! I instantly cried,
"My last crust of bread with these chaps I'll
    divide."
His majesty smiled, for he knew that I lied,
        He read all the thoughts in my mind.

I threw off my coat, to my cudgel held fast,
"Vengeance!" I cried, "for the days that are
    passed—
The road you chaps trod has an ending at last,
        Now I am commencing my reign"—
Rap, tap, at the door, I awoke with a bound,
The "Caller's" rich brogue through my noddle
    did sound:
"Och, Shandy, avick! shure its time you got
    round,
        And don't be delaying your train!"

A COLD WATER LYRIC.

Let others sing of vintage prime,
    Sparkling brightly in the cup;
Imported from each sunny clime,
    For eating manhood's vitals up;
But I will tune my harp to praise,
In unpremeditated lays,
That self-denying, noble band,

Of honest heart and friendly hand ;
Who founded an asylum here,
To dry the mourner's bitter tear,
And preach the gospel of reform,
That will domestic hearths keep warm ;
Those pioneers of envied fame,
    Who raised the temperance banner high,
And on its folds engrossed each name,
    To float beneath Oswego's sky.

'Tis not in legislative halls,
    Surrounded by the bay'nets gleam,
'Tis not in fierce, politic brawls,
    Can be dispelled the drunkard's dream.
Experience teaches us too true,
Coersive measures will not do.
We've heard the prohibition cry
Some candidates have raised on high ;
How *they* would send us steel-clad laws,
To guard our noble temperance cause,
With legislative bay'nets, too,
To slaughter all the drunken crew !

There is a saying in that isle
    Across the sea, where I have trod ;
And where oppressed ones with a smile
    Put all their hopes and trust in God—
"*Nabocklish**" sure, it is the trade

---

* Never mind them.

Of all reformers whom we sent,
Soon as their fortune we had made,
  To sell us out in parliament.

But here's to those, I fill the glass
  To overflowing from the spring,
And round, my boys, the toast will pass,
  In praise of all whom I do sing;
The brawny sons of hardy toil,
The noble lords of ev'ry soil,
The men of rough, untutor'd mind,
Possessed of jewels unrefined;
Each one endowed with nature's fire;
My humble Muse would fain aspire
To trace the thoughts, that unexpress'd,
Lie sleeping 'neath each russet vest;
Those noble boys who raised the flag—
No mean, dilapidated rag,—
But twined around with mem'ries bright,
Augmenting ev'ry Monday night,
As we in weekly councils meet,
And with fraternal smiling greet,
Each penitent who joins the van,
Resolved to be a sober man.
Then here's to them, fill ev'ry glass
  To overflowing from the spring;
And round, my boys, the toast shall pass,
  In praise of all whom I did sing.

EXIT SEVENTY-FOUR.

One evening, indulging in fond reveries,
Or building air-castles, whichever you please,
For know you, dear reader, I build with a will
My castles in latest of modern skill;
No sooner erected, my queen on her throne,
Than down they come, tottering, stone after
    stone.
That night I sat building, the hour was late,
The fire was flickering low in the grate,
I arose to replenish, when lo! what a sight
Met my wondering gaze, put my heart in a fright!
Unannounced in the room stood a man on whose
    brow
Old age had ruthlessly cut with his plow
Deep furrows and wrinkles, decrepit and old,
    And hoary indeed, was the look of the stranger.
He shiver'd and shook with rheumatics and cold,
    And looked the reverse to inspire me with
    danger.

"Who are you?" He answered: "I'm Seventy-
    Four."
    "The devil!" I cried, in amazement and wonder;
"Why did'nt you knock when you came to the
    door?"
    "I did," he replied, "hammered louder than
    thunder.

I thought you were dead, but I found you were
    dreaming,
So cozy and snug, with the fire on you beaming;
Quit dreaming, my boy, or you'll find if you joke
Too much with the fire, you'll encounter some
    smoke.
I was loath to depart, 'tis the truth that I tell,
Till I came to embrace you and bid you farewell."
"To receive your embraces 'tis not my desire;
Your sex isn't suited to Shandy Maguire—
And, know you, old codger, 'tis little I care
How soon you set sail through the snow-laden
    air.
I'm just as you found me a twelve-month ago,
    Still poor, discontented, downhearted and
        lonely;
Up life's rugged grades I am clambering slow,
    Just running on time to my meeting points
        only."

"That's why," he exclaimed, "I have called here
    to-night;
    Your wrongs in the past I have closely scanned
        over;
Ere parting, I mean to adjust them all right,
    And leave you behind me knee deep in rich
        clover."
"Sit down here beside me my worthy old friend,

I knew my misfortunes were near at an end;
You're a beautiful, youthful, and kindhearted
    man,"
Some moments the blarney profusely ran.
His features assumed a paternal glow,
As thus he addressed me, distinctly and slow.
His voice, patriarchial, did many times fail,
Recounting this brief, chronological tale:

"The worthy Grand Chief Engineer of the earth
    Proclaimed from His home beyond planet or
      star,
That I should commence at the moment of birth
Uniting mankind, smoothing factions that jar.
I traveled the globe on the wings of the storm,
I labored in vain the command to perform.
In castle and cot in all climes have I been,
In palace and prison sad sights have I seen;
Through highways and byways too many by
    name,
'Twas man against man, yes, and woman the
    same.
Each bloated oppressor, with miserly hoard,
Still clings to his gold, and God's poor are
    ignored;
Dissensions and quarrelings, in factions and
    creeds,
Bickerings, and wranglings, and damnable deeds.

The body politic's unsavory and sore,
Corruption has seized on its very heart's core.
Save noble exceptions, mankind I have found
Are guided by Satan the universe round.
I'll retire from the scene, my successor is near;
Perhaps he'll accomplish the mission next year.
To the B. of L. E. I've been partial, I own,
    There I found brothers who listen to reason,
· A man I triumphantly placed on the throne,
    Who'll shield you from danger and guard you
      from treason.

And now, my dear boy, I will gladden your heart
With something I'll whisper before I depart:
If you'll follow my counsels they'll lead you
    aright
To a clime where you'll dally in endless delight;
'Tis a land where vast wealth on the surface is
    found,
And companions, delighted, sport all the year
    round"—
"Oh, bless you!" I said, "will you tell me its
    name?"
    "You rascal" he cried, "do you mean to
    deceive me?"
"I do not, indeed, but my heart's in a flame,
    To hear where that climate's located, believe
    me."

His features assumed some incredible leers;
My eyes began shedding mock-penitent tears,
He saw them, again to his heart I went creeping,
Old men, like old maids, are soon conquered by
    weeping.

He resumed : "When your sails are all set to the
    breeze,
And off you go cruising in fanciful seas,
Remember directions I now shall unfold
You'll find they will lead to contentment and
    gold ;
Draw nearer, my life is fast ebbing away,
I'm nearing the dawn of eternity's day"—
The clock began tolling, my guest gave a bound;
    To stop him some moments I made an endeavor;
'Twas midnight, and scarcely had struck the
    twelfth sound,
    When Seventy-Four left my vision forever.

THE GOOD TIME COMING.

"Now freights are up," said Mickey Joyce,
    "And wages too, so boss, less lip;
Close reef your shrill, commanding voice,
    Or I'll be off and make a trip.
A life ashore is drudge and drive,

For twelve long hours, to and fro;
It matters not how hard I strive,
   I ne'er can get a watch below."

But freights are up and times are good,
   And owners very freely boast
"They'll give their 'Matlows' wholesome food,
   Roast beef, plum-duff, with quail on toast."
Just like the good old days of yore,
   When tables groaned with flesh and fish;
And captains brought their crews ashore,
   To find a still more dainty dish!

I yet can shift a sheet and hand
   A sail when equinoctials howl;
Besides, at sea, not like the land,
   The mates don't care how much I growl;
But here its work the live-long day,
   In ev'ry kind of stormy weather,
And scarcely get sufficient pay
   To keep my body and soul together.

Yourself and I have shipmates been
   Some twelve or thirteen years ago,
With Parsons, in the Algerine,
   Who gave us watch and watch below;
You then could growl as well as me,

And work "Tom Coxs' traverse*" too,
And on a first-class jamboree
    I never got the start of you.

For seven years I've done my best
    Against head seas and heavy gales;
'Twas 'full and by,' no ease nor rest;
    With stranded gear and tatter'd sails.
But now the wind is piping fair,
    And freights are on the rise once more;
Don't drive me or the yards I'll square,
    And on my lee leave jobs ashore.

I simply quote Mike's words to prove
    That times are on the mend again;
That freights and ships are on the move,
    To cheer the hearts of sailor men.
Old tars begin to roll their hips,
    And talk of all their pleasures past,
With captains, who commanded ships,
    And used them well before the mast.

---

* In nautical parlance, working " Tom Coxs' traverse " means to shirk
from duty.

TO P. M. ARTHUR.

Grand Chief Engineer of the Brotherhood of Locomotive Engineers,
Cleveland, Ohio.

My worthy chief, a word or two,
An humble friend will have with you,
   With no intent to flatter.
My Muse is honest, frank and blunt,
In manhood's fight she seeks the front,
   And can't be hired to spatter
High-sounding words of fulsome praise
On men who seek dark, devious ways,
   She does detest such clatter;
That's why, to-night, in accents true,
She whispers me to write to you,
   And so I jingle at her.

A general, you, of tactics rare,
Of toil you take the larger share,
   Your army all reviewing;
With honest words of hope and cheer,
You drive away all doubt and fear,
   Our grosser thoughts subduing.
'Tis better far, my worthy chief,
And in the end brings more relief
   From many ills accruing,
Than firing up each injured mind,
Until it is with passion blind,
   And conquered foes pursuing.

I often think, with keen delight,
Upon that last October night,
  When you and Greene together,
Surrounded by a faithful few
Good members of One-Fifty-Two—
  Both pictured stormy weather,
For any man who'd dare to yield
Our Brotherhoods' protecting shield
  For sly, official blether—
Who'd step within the slimy snare
Of promises, so seemly fair,
  Then bound by such a tether.

You have your faults, I know they're few,
You'll surely meet temptation, too,
  If not you're more than human;
Your duty calls you face to face
With men who are a purse-proud race,
  And full of keen acumen;
But, sure, your honest manly heart,
Will never from those maxims part,
  All prized so much by you, man.
Your life's a page where men can read,
And in temptation's hour, indeed,
  We know you proved a true man.

With weapons made of voice and pen,
You beard the lion in his den,

Unawed by fear or favor,
Our rights determined to maintain,
Each nerve you'll put to fullest strain,
        Regardless of palaver
From oily tongues, thrown out to woo
The mighty influence of you
        For any base enslaver.
Ah! well they know your cause is just,
And in our cause your knightly thrust
        Grows braver, still, and braver.

Then strike—but not below the belt—
Strike! your blows will soon be felt,
        Your aim is sure and steady,
Strike, and make each tyrant reel,
Strike! your words cut worse than steel,
        Fluent, fierce and ready.
Strike the hireling, knavish pack, '
Strike! an army's at your back,
        Patient, cool, unheady,
Waiting to sustain their Chief,
And drive our enemies to grief,
        In retribution's eddy.

5

A PEN PICTURE.

My mother, in juvenile years of her son,
Would say in a passion and sometimes in fun :
"Arrah Shandy, you rascal, your gostering tricks
Will get both yourself and your friends in a fix,"
And now, my dear *Journal*, I see an array
Of questions just out in the number for May,
Which bring to my mind the hard words of my
 mother,
Prophesying my friends both confusion and
 bother.

Your replies, I infer, satisfied the demand,
For which in exchange 1 extend you the hand
Of a rollicksome, careless, unfortunate elf,
Who will "rise and explain" a few words for
 himself.
Your answers were really too partial to me,
But *mine* shall be outspoken, candid and free—
An answer in future to all who'll enquire
And seek an acquaintance with Shandy Maguire.

In regard to my engine and what she can do,
That "writer" I'll answer, my words shall be few,
Because he don't care if I'm posted at all,
He wants us to think that himself knows it all.
Suffice it to say when the pay car comes round

No handier boy with the pen can be found ;
My autograph then with a flourish and dash
I'll exchange in return for some hard-earned cash.

You'll find me an honest gossoon I must say,
So long as temptation is kept from my way ;
I am truthful and never a lie will I tell,
If the truth, at the moment, will answer as well.
I am pious, and spend many hours in prayer,
When I stand on the rough, ragged edge of despair;
Much addicted to drinking, the bottles I drain,
When the corks go a-popping from Fancy's
    Champagne.

I can palm off a pun and occasional joke,
I can always enjoy a good sociable smoke ;
And dear to my heart is my colored dudeen
Which I sport in the band of my greasy caubeen.
My hair doesn't curl because in my youth,
I always would suffer for telling the truth ;
Besides, there's a saving in needles and thread
To mothers who toy with their sons by the head.

In size I am rather "betwixt and between,"
In looks I'm pronounced "most decidedly green."
Conversing—ah! then they exclaim : "What a
    rogue,
Sure he tickles my heart with his elegant brogue."
In dress, rather plain, and my wardrobe is light,

Not such as will gladden a landlady's sight;
When obliged to change quarters I move all my
    stock
In a trunk which I make from a well worn sock.

Few friends have I had, yet in smiles and in tears,
I have scrambled along to maturity's years;
And I fear I am doomed a "superfluous man"
To linger my days with the bachelor clan.
I am last of my race—when I'm summoned away,
When my mortal remains shall be lowered in
    clay,
No kindred will then be found kneeling in prayers,
Giving thanks for a death that has made them
    all heirs.

Now, ladies, I fear I have ruined for life
Ev'ry chance in my favor for getting a wife;
I have painted my picture with pen, ink and
    paper,
Well aware 'tis a foolish, ridiculous caper.
I conformed to rules I was taught in my youth,
When questions are asked my replies shall be
    truth;
I hope such a straight-forward course you'll
    admire,
And smile an approval on Shandy Maguire.

      *   *   *   *   *   *   *   *

Dear "Roger" whoever, wherever you are,

Your poem has caused me both grief and despair;

That bouncing grass widow has threatened to
      come

Along with her offspring in search of a home;

Since reading your reasons, she writes me they're
      true.

Please take her yourself—with such objects in
      view—

I fear you're the husband she waits for in tears,

And had cause for deserting herself and her
      dears.

"Garryowen" my regards, my long silence
      excuse,

Be prepared when I call for an overland cruise;

You were also invited—with prosperous weather

We'll both of us start for Kentucky together.

When your canvas is bent and you're ready to
      sail,

To Oswego, New York, send a letter by mail;

Once more 'neath the shade of magnolias I'll
      rhyme,

And escape for a season this winter-bound clime.

LOSS OF THE SCHOONER "I. G. JENKINS"

On Lake Ontario, off Oswego, November, 1875. Read at the Benefit
Entertainment in behalf of the Widows and Orphans.

Oswego in garments of mourning is clad,
  She weeps for her gallant and brave,
Who were summoned away to the ranks of the
    dead,
  'Neath Ontario's foam-crested wave.
All as brave as ere trod fore and aft on the deck;
  We have known them from infancy's years;
And their doom we can tell by the fragments of
    wreck
  That are washed by the seas to our piers.

Oh, hark to the news which prevails on each
    street,
  Through the highways and byways 'tis tossed,
In a grief-laden tone, from each person we meet,
  All proclaiming the Jenkins is lost!
"She went down with all hands," is the pitiful
    cry
  Sent from hearts unaccustomed to weep,
With the tears in a flood rolling free from each
    eye,
  As a tribute to those in the deep.

All her sailors were brave as ere climbed up a
    spar,

And her mates they were made to command;
Captain Brown was as noble and skillful a tar
    As ever sailed off from the land.
Such were the men whom her owners could boast,
But clouds wore a dark, angry frown,
Which obscured all the land marks surrounding
    · our coast,
    On the morning the Jenkins went down.

A merciless gale o'er Ontario's breast
    Was driving with terrible force,
It had a full sweep from the stormy nor'west,
    And drove her away from her course.
All human exertions to save her, we know,
    Were made by her captain and crew;
Alas! all in vain, for the gale-driven snow
    Our lighthouse shut out from their view.

Hear the cries of the widows and orphans arise
    To-night on the cold biting air.
Oh! how hard is the heart that's unmoved by
    the sighs
    And the symbols of deepest despair;
The husbands and fathers who labored for bread,
    Are rolling in watery graves,
Never more to arise till the trump of the dead
    Shall call them from under the waves.

All you who are blessed with affluence and
    wealth,
  Who bask in prosperity's ray,
Whose lives are a round of contentment and
    health,
  To you for assistance we pray.
Oh! pity the wives of the ill-fated tars,
  Give freely from plentiful stores,
Their husbands, perhaps, may be lashed to the
    spars,
And come washed by the seas to our doors.

AN ALBUM RHYME.

Dear *Journal:* A lady one evening I met,
A valued acquaintance, a handsome brunette;
A frolicsome, fun-loving, beautiful creature,
Exquisitely molded in every feature.
Like most of her sex of the beautiful type,
Whose natural charms are lusciously ripe,
She had scores of admirers all " willing to die,"
So they madly exclaimed, "for a glance of her
    eye."

A favorite song for myself she would sing,
When turning her music I noticed a ring,
That spoke of engagement; I saw at a glance

My chances were slim, so I woke from my trance.
That tell-tale said plainly she'd never be mine,
Henceforth like a slave I will kneel at her
    shrine,
And blarney her up in as elegant style,
As any gossoon from the Emerald Isle.

That evening I saw she'd an object in view,
She said : " There's a leaf in my album for you,
And, this for a subject: 'please tell what you
    see
To admire in a wild, naughty girl like me.' "
She smiled at my glances, she gave me her hand,
It thrilled like the touch of a magical wand,
It put me in rapture as well as in rhyme,
And here's the response which I sent in due
    time :

I see—but, alas ! I'm deserving of pity
Because all my wishes are hopeless, dear Kittie,
I see a profusion of dark wavy tresses,
Two lips that were made to receive my caresses,
Lips that the tint of vermillion disclose,
Tinged with the hue we admire in the rose,
Eyes that can pierce through my soul with their
    brightness,
Hands that out-rival the lily in whiteness,
A bust that is rounded perfectly by nature,

Proclaiming the owner a beautiful creature,

A voice that is sweeter than tropic birds winging

Their way through rich gardens of melody,
    singing,

Smiles that enrapture my senses when gazing,

More bright than the Sun when in splendor he's
    blazing,

A breath that surpasses the sweet-morning dew,
    love,

Or fragrance that blooms 'round the shores of
    Peru, love.

Right here I should cease, but an imp at my
    shoulder

Keeps whispering : " time all those charms will
    moulder,"

And now while aglow in the noon of your youth,
    love,

I give you advice to be taken forsooth, love,

" Lay·siege to a heart that you know will not
    falter

Performing the vows which are made at the
    altar,

Don't mind his appearance, if brawny his form,

So best when he buffets adversity's storm.

His coat—what's the odds if its torn and tat-
    tered ?

His hat may from service be crownless and
    battered,
When married, he'll quickly improve with your
    aid, love,
Besides, he will not let you die an old maid, love."
"Will you take this advice which I tender to you,
    love?
Of course, if you do, you are welcome to, true love.
Don't answer me "no" or you'll weep it in sorrow,
If "yes" you can dance at our wedding to-mor-
    row."

TO DOCTOR LAWRENCE REYNOLDS.

(EX-CITY PHYSICIAN.)

Dear Doctor: I'm rather inclined to the notion
    That things haven't went as they really should
      go,
To pay for the years of untiring devotion
    You gave to the cause, both in sunshine and
      snow.
God knows when we made you a City Physician,
    With pay just sufficient to furnish you grub,
We never supposed they'd create a commission,
    And knock out your brains with an Albany
      club.

Alas ! like yourself, there are many brave fellows,
  Whose features have lengthened a fathom or
    more ;
All sad, disappointed, downhearted Othellos,
  Washed high on the rocks of despondency's
    shore.
Experience has taught all those boys to their
    sorrow,
  That labor don't always receive its full pay—
That birds left to fly in the fields till to-morrow
  May laugh at the cage and float gaily away.

God bless the good times that have left us forever,
  When candidates smilingly walked on the
    street ;
With speeches well studied, so oily and clever,
  And asked us to drink ev'ry time that we'd
    meet.
Then meekly request us to help them to office ;
  Oh Lord ! how they'd make us the promises
    fair,
But doctor, avick ! they would break them and
    scoff us,
  When once they'd sit down in an Alderman's
    Chair.

And there they've been sitting for years and
    been sleeping

On nice cushioned chairs, in our grand City
    Hall,
Whilst charter amendments went stealthily
    creeping
    Around through the flesh-pots, and gobbled
    them all.
They left not a bone worth the labor of picking;
    Our dear city daddies we well may reproach.
Hereafter, we'll leave them to do their own
    kicking,
    Because they are like the fifth wheel to a coach.

Oh, times they have changed since High Joints
    came in fashion,
    And those are the boys who may whistle and
    sing,
How slyly they work—not a loud word in passion
    When grinding the shears for an Alderman's
    wing.
We need not much care how our votes are con-
    tested,
    The voice of the many is drowned by the few,
And justice is shackled, confined, and arrested—
    Fifth warders well know what High Jointers
    can do.

But, Doctor, cheer up, for the day will come
    surely

When out on the war path we'll sally once
    more;
When those who are now back of breast works
    securely,
    Must come to the caucus the same as of yore;
And there, foot to foot, with our scalping knives
    ready,
        We'll square up accounts, and we'll soon end
        the strife;   .
Our aim will be deadly, unerring and steady,
    Defying your skill to recall them to life.

DEATH LEVELS ALL.

By the light of a glimmering taper
    Which scarce penetrated the gloom,
I perused in the evening paper,
    One night as I sat in my room,
How Archibald Perkins was lying
    Delirious and seriously ill,
His critical ailment defying
    The best of our medical skill.

"That's news!" I exclaimed, and the paper
    I threw on my tenantless bed.
I quickly extinguished the taper,
    Strange notions ran wild in my head.

I meant to secure an admission
  To the chamber where Archie was lying;
I could pass as a skillful physician
  And see how a rich man lay dying.

I entered and found him as lowly
  As any poor mortal could be;
. By efforts most painful he slowly
  Held short conversation with me;
I felt of his pulse and pretended
  I knew all about his complaint,
I told him to cure I intended,
  Altho' he was feeble and faint.

"In medical lore I am noted"—
  For killing far more than I cure—
Some jargon expressions I quoted,
  He thought I was skillful, I'm sure.
Faint hope o'er his features went flying:
  "Your name sir?" he then did enquire,
"Oh, one that can save you from dying,
  Yours truly, Lord Shandy Maguire."

The dying fool aped after titles,
  Supposing my high-sounding name
Would give a new lease to his vitals,
  And fan life's faint spark into flame.

" Your Lordship, " said he, "I am wealthy,
    When cured I'll one thousand allow."
I replied : "you're sufficiently healthy
    To give me your autograph now."

He mutter'd of business relations,
    Of stock-board transactions did prate,
Of shares and their latest quotations,   .
    And thirty days grace after date.
He prayed that the past be forgiven,
    And health with its blessings sent back,
Of living more closely to heaven.   ·
    I then screwed him down on the rack.

"I've often heard tell of a story,
    How Satan an angel would be
When ill, but again in his glory,
    The devil an angel was he ;
And now, since we're talking of devils,
    I have a few words I must say :
Quit thinking of all your past revels,
    And for your poor soul let us pray."

"You're now in a sinking condition,
    Not fit to respond to the call,
I'm neither a quack nor physician,
    Can give no assistance at all.

Great riches on earth you were given,
  For reasons I cannot explain;
You'll not find a passport to Heaven
  In all of your ill-gotten gain."

The Dives of this world are many,
  In luxury rolling secure,
And will not contribute a penny
  To save from starvation the poor;
But grind us through ages and ages,
  Till sinews are worn to thread,
Curtailing our lives and our wages,
  When fighting the battle for bread."

"You've always been fond of fast riding,
  And sorely the patience would try
Of slaves switched for hours on a siding
  Until you'd go thundering by;
You'll find previous running exceeded
  By speed most appaling to view,
To climes where no snow-plow is needed,
  To-night in old Charon's canoe."

Your eyes will soon close on your capers,
  Old death's at the head of your stairs,
To-morrow the news in the papers
  Will gladden the hearts of your heirs.

'Though my coat hangs by patches and
  stitches,
  My purse and my pockets are light,
Yet Archie, for all of your riches
  I wouldn't change places to-night.

MORE TROUBLE.

At the close of a wearisome day,
  My engine in round-house secured,
I was carelessly strolling away,
  Until called to "examine the board."
A feeling that all wasn't right
  Crept instantly over me there;
This order that burst on my sight
  Soon plunged me in deepest despair:

"On his arrival, with speed
  To headquarters send Shandy Maguire;
Have promptly this order obeyed,
  (Signed) Archibald Perkins, Esquire."
No wonder I gazed in dismay,
  With tears running down from each eye;
I thought Perkins was cold in clay,
  And his nose turned up to the sky.

I entered, and saw at a glance
  What my chances were going to be,
As round like a bear did he prance,
  With his eyes shooting vengeance at me.
I moistened the valves of my tongue,
  Kicked the office door shut with a slam,
Knowing well 'tis the same to be hung
  For a sheep as it is for a lamb.

"So, so, Mr. Shandy, you're here,
  Impostor, physician and quack,
"My Lord!" he exclaimed with a sneer,
  "Is *your body* prepared for the rack?
T'other night, with a hellish design,
  Concealed by the drapery's gloom,
You entered a chamber of mine,
  To hurry me off to the tomb.

"This letter I hold in my hand
  Will have you committed to jail,
For villainy skillfully plan'd,
  A crime not admitting of bail;
The best legal talent I've got,
  The laws shall be changed at my will;
I'll send you in dungeons to rot
  On the charge of attempting to kill."

"Shut off, and down brakes on your slang,
    Or if not, Mr. Archie you'll find,
From a painful, unmerciful bang,
    That muscle's more powerful than mind.
The odds are against you, old boy,
    Consider, your health is still poor,
And 'twould give me the greatest of joy
    To measure your length on the floor.

"The charge I fling back in your face.
    And of one thing I'm certain and sure :
You've the heart to bring shame and disgrace
    On a man just because he is poor :
But if fortune hops into the scales,
    And lingers awhile at our side,
As we scud with prosperity's gales,
    In your handsome gilt coach we shall ride.

"In His mercy God pity the man,
    Engaged in the struggles of life,
Who seeks on the laboring plan,
    Subsistence for children and wife.
It were better by far he was call'd
    In the morning of life, to the grave,
Than linger along to be gall'd
    By the fears of becoming a slave.

"By a move on the chess-board of war,
   Four millions of Blacks were made free;
Besides, you import from afar
   The rat-eating, heathen Chinee.
You move 'em all over this land,
   Check-mating our struggles for Right,
Ah, yes, with an iron-clad hand
   By Heavens, you'd shackle the white.

"How happy you'd feel, could you say,
   To the over-taxed laboring class,
'I am made of far daintier clay,
   To your knees, and bow down as I pass.'
But we'll never submit to be slaves
   While a pulse-throb of manhood remains;
As freedmen we'll sink in our graves,
   Ere breathing one hour in your chains.

"Then pause in your onward career;
   Reflect on the course you pursue,
Retribution, stalks close in the rear
   Of such hardened old wretches as you;
You'll meet with it, sooner or late,
   There's a terrible sentence in store,
When you pass through Eternity's gate,
   For the wrongs you inflict on the poor.

"I know that my head you'll lop off,
  You never *could* relish a joke,
So here is material enough,
  For your silver-gilt dudeen to smoke.
When the wreaths curl up round your nose,
  As you lay on your velvet settee,
Perhaps you'll be lull'd to repose
  By a fond recollection of me."

I ceased, and requested my pay,
  Supposing my service would end;
He order'd me mildly away,
  And said he would sentence suspend.
"Arrah, glory to Heaven, old boy,
  Give me hold of your fist ere we part,
And remember, kind words can send joy,
  Thrilling down to the depths of the heart.

———

THE FREAKS OF FORTUNE.

One evening I sat meditating
  On various ills we endure,
And many, indeed, are the ailments
  Encountered thro' life by the poor.

I heard a slow footstep approaching,
  And turning around in my chair
I saw an old man, on whose features
  Sat sorrow and hopeless despair.

He looked like a way-worn stranger.
  I did not his business enquire,
But asked him to come and be seated
  'Longside of myself at the fire.
He thanked me in accents of sorrow;
  His voice, Ah! I've heard it before.
'Twas Archibald Perkins, in tatters,
  Who came unannounced to my door!

Alas! what a change in poor Archie;
  Time was when he had at command
A gilt equipage, and his riches
  Were talked of all over the land.
His bearing, then chillingly haughty,
  Conceit played a prominent part;
I often have wondered if Heaven
  Created the man with a heart!

I heard he encountered misfortune,
  Was blown on adversity's rocks,
Because he endeavored to "corner"
  The market by watering stocks.

With prosperous sunbeams around him
His friends were a numerous clan,
But now—he was sad and forsaken—
A heart-broken, weary old man!

"Alas! I'm exhausted with hunger,"
Exclaimed my poor, ill-fated guest—
"I fain would implore you to grant me
Some needed refreshments and rest.
I trudged many miles since the morning,
I'm seeking a place to lie down,
Wherein I'll escape for a season
The force of Adversity's frown."

"Benumbed with fatigue and exposure,
I ask you in charity's name,
To grant me this night in seclusion;
No more from your pity I'll claim.
To-morrow I'll leave you forever,
This night in your town is my last;
The rest of my life I'll endeavor
To make some amends for the past."

He ceased, and I stood up before him,
To notice the look of his eye.
I paused for a moment, reflecting
On how I should make him reply.

Poor Archie, a tramp and a beggar!
   Who once had a palace-car train;
With waiters to fan him and feed him,
   And pour him out choicest Champagne!

"Indeed I am more than astonished
   To see you so friendless and poor.
I scarcely could credit my senses,
   When first you arrived at my door.
You're quite a professional beggar,
   You've learned the trade very fast;
You're weak as that mem'rable evening
   You thought you were breathing your last.

"Before I will grant you the favor
   You earnestly seek and desire,
A little account must be settled
   Between you and Shandy Maguire.
I hope sir you haven't forgotten
   Those truths which I told you of yore,
That brokers and breakers of Wall Street,
   Would toss you on poverty's shore.

" Remember the time you sat grinding
   The hearts of poor, laboring men,
By orders tyranic'lly issued,
   Each day by a dash of your pen;

Your cutting and slashing of wages,
  Your payment in scrip, and the mode
Of testing our power of endurance
  Along the whole line of the road.

"Oh, Heaven! my wrath is unbounded,
  At how you abused ev'ry crew
In days when the gavel was sounded
  By such an old tyrant as you.
'Twas seldom, if ever, you granted
  Redress from each heartless decree.
No doubt, you distinctly remember
  Suspending a sentence on me.

" Yourself graduated from labor,
  But beggars on horseback excel,
They drive right ahead in their fury,
  And ride through the portals of—Well,
I can't see the use of me marring
  My beautiful face with a frown.
Besides, I have never assisted
  In kicking a man when he's down.

"You're hungry! sit down at this table,
  You're not quite so choice as you were
In days when the stock holders dined you
  And fed you on sumptuous fare ;

Because you reduced the expenses,
  By making more work for less pay;
And telling them how you could run us
  As far as you chose for a day."

I ceased, and I quickly regretted
  My rashness to one of his years.
He bowed o'er his head and I noticed,
  His eyes were fast filling with tears.
"Ha, ha! my old sport, I discover
  My words have struck deep in their force
And reached away down to that fountain
  Well known by the name of 'remorse.'"

"Perhaps you are playing impostor,
  Arrayed in that mendicant garb,
To see with what vengeance I'll prick you
  To-night with my merciless barb;
The morrow's bright sun may behold you
  Once more at the head of affairs,
Arrayed in rich broad-cloth, and all of
  Your old time original airs."

"Here's bread, you can see I've no butter,
  Nice dainties to us are a treat;
This bone affords excellent picking
  To furnish a morsel of meat.

Here's hay-seed some time I've had steeping;
    My grocery-man sells it for tea;
The sugar and cream are dispensed with,
    Since wages were slaughtered on me.

"Some more I will do to console you,
    And soothe you for days that have fled,
When supper is over I'm ready
    To give you the half of my bed;
Because I'm inclined to consider
    Your bark was far worse than your bite.
Eat hearty now, Archie, poor fellow!
    You'll not leave my cabin to-night."

OUR LETTER CARRIERS.

Once more the onward march of time,
    In measured tread, from pole to pole.
Through every land, in every clime,
    Has marked again the seasons roll
That brings the festive days, when Mirth
    Will reign supreme in joyous cheer,
And every heart o'er all the earth
    Will welcome give the young New Year.

This is the time we recognize
　The faithful service of the past,
We march along with glad surprise
　To those, 'mong whom our lots are cast;
Bestowing there a gift of love,
　Rewarding with an open hand—
We sow the seed we'll reap above,
　When called to join Jehovah's band.

Of all who may our bounty claim
　A few stand first amid the throng ;
A faithful Band, unknown to fame,
　Who are the heroes of my song,
Who plod along their toilsome way,
　In Summer sun, or Winter sleet,
From early morn till close of day,
　On steady and untiring feet.

Oh !　Who can tell the news they bear,
　As on they hurry to and fro,
The tender joy, or grim despair,
　The written tale of weal or woe.
The human heart may surge and sway
　With varied tidings that they leave,
As on they travel every day,
　To bid us all rejoice, or grieve.

Such servants we can ne'er despise,
   We'll prove each faithful action here;
We will reward and recognize
   At this the dawning of the year.
We'll cheer their hearts and urge them on
   Upon their daily toilsome way
And ere the dawn of Eighty-One,
   They will our gen'rous gifts repay.

LAKE MICHIGAN.

The chain of lakes are rough indeed,
   And fearful sometimes to behold;
When chilling winds prevail in speed,
   And drive along the biting cold;
More fearful yet than all the rest,
   The very first in danger's van,
Is this, the great lake of the West,
   'Tis term'd "Wild Lake Michigan."

The shores, like mountains steep and high,
   Are all composed of crumbling sand;
If underneath a wreck does lie
   One man in ten may chance to land.

No friendly branch or root projects
    To clamber from the rolling waves,
Kind Heaven alone is all protects
    Poor shipwrecked tars from watery graves.

And yet I love the billows wild,
    When lashed by winds and capped with foam,
When mountain waves on waves are piled,
    That seem to touch heav'n's cloudy dome;
Then downward sink in valleys deep,
    Of mad'ning, swirling, dashing spray,
Until, rebounding, on they sweep
    In unobstructed force away.

THE COMING OF SPRING.

A few short weeks will make a change,
    Important in our town,
When moral laws will take effect,
    And vice be trampled down;
When hoary Frost will take his leave
    Of every hill and plain;
And smiling Spring, the poor man's hope,
    With us once more will reign.

The merchant's safe he'll then unlock
　To con his dollars o'er,
And then invest judiciously,
　In hope of gaining more;
The wheels of enterprise shall hum,
　Which long inactive staid,
When those much looked for days shall come,
　To give new life to trade.

And we who must by labor live
　Will hail the joyous sound;
Our willing hands we'll freely give,
　To make the air resound.
With steady din of work restored,
　When all may laugh and sing,
To know dull times, so much deplored,
　Shall vanish with the Spring.

———

TO AN IMPORTUNATE CONTRIBUTOR.

Dear Madam :—With feelings of sadness,
　I'm forced to address you in rhyme;
Your letters will drive me to madness,
　Unless you repent of the crime.

At first, when I thought you were joking,
  I sent you soft nonsense galore,
But, madam, of late you're provoking,
  And piercing my heart to the core.

The "gush" that's contained in each letter,
  Your mode of describing your charms;
Your hope, that for worse or for better,
  I'll linger my life in your arms.
So "gentle, kind-hearted and loving,"
  An angel you'd have me believe,
Whose husband at present is roving
  All over the land on "French leave."

You never have written the reason
  He fled from his lodging and board;
His meals—were they ready in season?
  In jars did you have the last word?
Have you read of a woman called "Caudle?"
  (Would that all Mrs. Caudles were hung.)
Now, say, did your husband skedaddle
  Away from your musical tongue?

You've asked for my true name so often,
  I'll answer, don't think me a liar,
May my eyes be stone blind in my coffin,
  If my name isn't Shandy Maguire.

7

The ladies in youth called me "Candy,"
  Because I was sweet—what a shame
That mother should change it to Shandy,
  Hence, madam, my "comical name."

You've two little cherubs, you write me,
  Both handsome, the same as their ma,
Whose juvenile tricks will delight me,
  When once I'm installed as their pa.
Oh! know you, dear madam, I'd rather,
  One thousand times sooner, I swear!
Have one of my own call me "father,"
  Than scores like your beautiful pair.

Your eyes, they are black, and what matter?
  I care not a fig for their hue;
It never puts meat on the platter,
  Be the shade black or heavenly blue;
Were you and I coupled together,
  Your husband then chance to come back,
I'm certain, dear madam, that either
  Or both of our eyes would be black.

The poor devil sighed for his freedom,
  Like many another, I know,
Whose wrongs do impulsively lead 'em
  On roving commissions to go.

He dreamt in his youth and his fond age
  Of angels, and conjugal vows,
But awoke to confinement and bondage,
  And petticoat rule in his spouse.

Because in my rhymes I feel jolly,
  And conjure a smile to the face,
Don't think, from my capers and folly,
  I sigh for your absent love's place:
I'm sure it is better to tarry
  And die an old bachelor, too,
Than take any chances, and marry
  A bouncing "grass widow" like you.

A widow, plump, fair and kind-hearted,
  In garments of mourning arrayed,
Whose husband from life has departed,
  I'd marry as soon as a maid..
When cold, icy blasts would sweep o'er us,
  Companioned by direst alarms,
I'd laugh at the wrath of old Boreas,
  And weather the gale in her arms.

So your hair is an auburn color,
  In ringlets adorning your head ;
I'll wager my life to one dollar
  Your hair is a carroty red.

If you stood on a curve, and a stranger,
  The lever I'd quickly throw back,
And I'd think you a signal of danger,
  Dropped off from some train on the track.

Were you ever possessed of a father?
  If so, for his sake will you cease?
Have you ever been blessed with a mother?
  If you were, in her name grant me peace.
Your sisters and brothers, if any,
  I hope will advise you to pause ;
At present our jails have too many
  Like you, for transgressing the laws.

Now madam, I pray you, give over ;
  Have patience, at least till we're sure
Your husband lies under the clover,
And then we can slumber secure.
Don't let my "droll warbling" allure you,
  To be my "heart's queen" don't aspire,
For you'll not find a fool, I assure you,
  In him who's called Shandy Maguire.

TO R. F. LEFFIN, MOBILE, ALA.

Ah, Bob, my old friend, as the snow-flakes are
 flying,
 I pen you these lines at Ontario's shore ;
Perhaps you'll peruse them, contentedly lying,
 Where Nature too partially squanders her
 store ;
Where song birds melodiously sing in the bowers,
 And mocking birds whistle their notes on each
 tree,
Where love-tales are whispered thro' pathways
 of flowers ;
 Ah, those are the scenes that are treasured by
 me.

Enjoy them, my friend, but in moments of leisure,
 Remember the days that have fled long ago ;
Yes, think of the days and the evenings of pleasure
 We sported together where gulf breezes blow.
This life is a lease, you must sing and be jolly,
 Bob, quaff the full bowl of enjoyment to-day,
To-morrow old Care may set brakes on your folly,
 And stall you, my boy, in the midst of your
 play.

Oh, often, I think, 'tis a dire occupation
 We follow, in order to gain us our bread ;
"He died at his post," is a poor consolation,

To steal from our graves and peruse when
  we're dead ;
1 only can speak for the son of my mother,
  And tell you " such honors I really decline,"
Ah, yes ; and I think Bob, I know of one other
  Whose answer would be in such language as
  mine.

Consider the dangers that hourly beset us ;
  A wheel's revolution may end our career.
Tho' brave be our acts, our officials forget us
  When mangled, and slaughtered, and cold on
  our bier.
We never have learned that Boards of Directors
  Donate the poor widows so much by the year,
Nor yet have we known them as orphans' pro-
  tectors,
  Rewarding the acts of a brave engineer.

A switch may be wrong or a bridge may be rotten,
  A trestle but poorly constructed, and fall,
Orders be loosely obeyed or forgotten,
  And trains may be met without orders at all ;
A tire may burst or a boiler go crashing,
  The rods and the pins into pieces may fly,
A rail may be broken, and send us on dashing,
  Unshrived to the Court of our Maker, on high.

But Bob, here's a truce to each gloomy foreboding,
    Away from such thoughts you and I must
    retreat.
A laugh conquers Care, when our hearts he's
    corroding,
    There's time to shake hands with old Nick when
    we meet.
Bad luck to his black, smoky phiz, we defy him,
    His old cloven foot you and I cannot scare,
With guns double-shotted, if ever we spy him,
    We'll riddle his carcass with broadsides of
    prayer.

Your lady love gives me a glance full of meaning,
    As much as to say, "My poor heart is in pain,"
The dregs of despair I am sure she is draining,
    And gladly she'd hail your return Bob, again,
'Tis sad to behold the dear girl bewailing
    Her lover, who's far, far away from her view.
Sooner than see her health rapidly failing,
    Old friend, I will court her by proxy for you.

No doubt you are still flirting gayly with Nettie,
    Who lives in the rose-trellised cot at Spring
    Hill ;
Who strolled at your side down the beach to
    Frascatti,

And floated all night in the waltz and quadrille.
And, oh, the delight coming home from the party!
    When weary, up close to your arms she would
        creep;
And kisses you'd steal by the hundred, my hearty,
    As soundly the darling pretended to sleep.

Regards to the boys who of yore congregated
    Where mirth and her minions hold carnival
        still;
A sigh for our brothers whose lives were ill-fated,
    Ah, light be the turf on Cole, Quigley and Hill.
And now, you'll remember I hold you my debtor,
    I hope you'll devote me an evening or two.
I'll gladly peruse all the news from a letter
    That's penned in the South by a "Snow Bird"
        like you.

———

THE CLERGY ON HELL.

The clergy are now agitating the word,
    The Bible is ransacked all 'round,
Fierce thunder from pulpits, on all sides is heard,
    Proclaiming where hell can be found.
Orthodoxy declares it a bottomless pit,
    Overflowing with brimstone and fire,
Where millions on millions, must roast on a spit,
    Impaled by God's merciless ire.

Each preacher he fashions a hell of his own,
  To suit both the age and the clime,
God prosper their labor, we'll leave them alone,
  They're having a hell-roaring time.
I enter the list of explorers and claim,
  To know all its bearings right well;
What's more, these few lines are inspired by the
    flame,
  And the fearful surroundings of hell.

Right here on this earth as it travels thro' space,
  From equator away to the polls,
I freely maintain is that terrible place,
  Where we suffer in bodies and souls.
We.existed before, but in some other sphere,
  Some planet remote in the sky,
Where for leading a reckless and sinful career,
  We were kicked from that region on high.

We starving down here were the rich ones up
    there,
  Who clung to our miserly hoard,
Every beggar we see was some proud millionaire,
  Whom the wants of his fellows ignored;   .
And those on this earth with their pockets well
    lined,
  With all the good things which we love,

The merciful God of creation designed,
    That they were the beggars above.

We are now the reverse of what once we have
    been,
    And you know the old saying right well :
" Put a beggar on horse-back he'll never draw
    rein
    'Till he rides through the portals of hell ; "
Fast horses we rode up above, but we rolled
    In the shape of a babe on this earth,
And our first tiny squall did the sad tale unfold,
    Where we entered the moment of birth.

When our flesh is all purged, and this pilgrimage
    o'er,
    Our remains will be laid in the tomb ;
And from there we'll ascend to our riches once
    more,
    Far away from this valley of gloom.
There the rich ones of earth for subsistence must
    fight,
    They must struggle in bondage and strife,
And we beggars will dally in endless delight,
    If we only can think of this life.

KITTIE, DEAR.

Now the summer days are dying,
And the leaves will soon be flying,
When the chilling winds come hieing,
Kittie, dear,
All our pleasure trips are over,
That we made through scented clover,
Since you chose me as your lover,
Kittie, dear.

All the hours we strolled together,
In the glorious sunny weather,
With our hearts as light as feather,
Kittie, dear,
Have been full of untold blisses,
Sighs, and vows, and humid kisses,
With you, fairest of young misses.
Kittie, dear.

Soon the snow-flakes will be falling,
And the cold intense, appalling,
And my heart for yours be calling,
Kittie, dear.
Now I think 'tis time to marry,
Or my hopes may all miscarry,
If you longer wish to tarry,
Kittie, dear.

We are young and both true-hearted,
And upon life's road we're started;
Let us wed and ne'er be parted,

               Kittie, dear.

While we've health we're full of treasures;
We'll have joy in flowing measures,
And our share of wedded pleasures,

               Kittie, dear.

Ah! that smile is answer dearly,
And it speaks in tones sincerely;
Better thus than tell me tearly,

               Kittie, dear.

Time will make our hearts grow fonder;
In the future days we'll wander,
And on scenes like this we'll ponder,

               Kittie dear.

THE CLAM BAKE.

Held on the Beach, near the Dorlan House, Norwalk, Ct., October 22, 1875.

Since first in very tender age
I made my bow on Nature's stage
To act my part, and fill the plan
That God assigns to every man;
Since first I heard, in accents loud,
The plaudits of the merry crowd,

I ne'er before did feel such joy
Of moments pure, without alloy,
As when I stood before the throng,
An honored bard of simple song,
On Norfolk's beach, where mirth held sway,
One ne'er-to-be-forgotten day ;
Where tables all were freighted down,
   And every indication bore
That plenty would our banquet crown
   With choicest gifts of sea and shore.

From far Pacific's distant slope,
   Where rivers run o'er golden sands,
Came brothers full of life and hope,
   With noble hearts and friendly hands.
From Maine, where fierce Atlantic's roar
Re-echoes on her rock-bound shore,
Came representatives along,
With words of cheer to swell the throng.
The Canadas, in regions North,
Sent many noble offspring forth,
Whose honest features impress bore
Of summer suns and winter's hoar.
From Dixie's land, whose name can thrill
The tender chords of memory still ;
Where tropic breezes waft perfume
Around her shore's perennial bloom,

Came brothers, sent with tidings grand
Of noble deeds in Dixie's land.
The North, the South, the West, the East,
Were represented at the Feast.
No niggard store, no miser's fare,
But choicest viands, rich and rare ;
As course on course did disappear,
Each new succeeding course was near,
Till appetite at last did say,
" Our hosts are victors here to-day. "
E'en then the remnant on the shore
Would feed as many mortals more.
As round these bounteous tables sate,
Within the Wooden-Nutmeg State.
Old ocean's depths were ransacked o'er,
To tempt our appetites on shore ;   .
And Neptune oft was forced to yield
The palm to forest, stream and field.
No epicure could ever wish
To taste a richer flavored dish ;
No banquet hall in olden time,
    When Rome her conquering flag unfurled,
Its equal spread throughout her clime,
    When reigning mistress of the world.

And, think you that I mean to slight,
    By silence, those divinely fair—

The galaxy of beauty bright—
  That deigned to grace that banquet there ?
And, think you, that my heart is cold,
And cast in rugged nature's mold ?
My eyes grown dim, obscured by haze,
And clouded o'er by lucre's blaze ?
Ah, no ! that dear enraptured thrill
Of early youth keeps bounding still.
When years accumulate on years ;
When hoary age brings groans and tears ;
When sluggish streams move through my veins
And scarce the breath of life remains ;
E'en then, in death's dark, dismal hour,
I'd own the sway of woman's power.
I only fear'd my skill to sing,
And make my harp responsive ring
To thoughts, whose sweet, resistless flow
Comes surging up from depths below,
Where woman steers by beauty's chart
Around the tendrils of my heart.
Her eyes are beacons, flashing bright,
  And when their beams encircle me,
I have no fear in darkest night
  To navigate life's stormy sea.

But one there was amongst the rest,
  A lady, eloquent and fair ;

A peerless queen in song and jest,
    With dreamy eyes and wavy hair.
Her words, evoking smiles or tears,
    Soon won their way through social bands,
And played as sweetly round our ears
    As harps when touched by angel hands.
And when the parting hour drew nigh,
    We there were 'thralled by beauty's spell,
The murmured words: "kind friends, good bye"
    The silvery tone : " farewell, farewell."

She left as left those angels bright,
    When summon'd off from mortal ken,
In dazzling rays of heavenly light,
    In olden time, from sons of men.

Kind benefactors, noble men !
    How may a man from labor's ranks
Employ a rude, untutor'd pen,
    To tender you our heartful thanks ?

My noble Chief, your pardon give,
    If for this moment I aspire
To be the Chief Executive
    Of brothers bred to danger dire ;
The men who foremost lead the van,
    Who first must feel the deadly shock ;

And who in trying moments can
   Stand firm, unflinching as the rock;
It is for those, that fearless throng,
   I fain would have my thanks resound,
I merely clothe in simple song
   Your words upon Long Island Sound.

Kind benefactors, now I pray,
   May life to you, and all your kin,
Be one continued cloudless ray,
   Where Fortune's smiles come teeming in;
And when life's evening draws a-nigh,
   When all must kiss the chast'ning rod,
May you to realms beyond the sky
   Be call'd, to dwell in peace with God.
'Tis not because of princely fare,
   Nor "Ninety's" speed o'er splendid track,
That swift, and safely, bore us there,
   And safe, and swiftly, brought us back.
Ah, no! but 'tis because you stand
   Where noble friends before you stood;
Who recognized throughout the land,
   Our noble, peerless Brotherhood.

But hark! I hear a mighty sound;
   'Tis circling near from States remote;
It makes the very earth resound,

8

As springing from one single throat ;
It is my brothers' thankful cry,
   Which hovers o'er my feeble pen ;
Twelve thousand tongues resounding high
   In one sincerely felt Amen.

CHRISTMAS.

Let the bells peal along,
   With vibrations of song,
On the clear frosty air of the night ;
   Let them sound in our ears,
   Till they banish our fears,
And our hearts feel the thrills of delight ;
   For old Christmas is here,
   And we greet it sincere ;
'Tis a time when we sit round the board ;
   Our dear friends from afar,
   Find the doors all ajar,
And the larder with good things well stored.

"Merry christmas !" we cry,
   And the glance of each eye
Is a sure indication of mirth ;
   Let the wassail bowl flow
   In the radiant glow,

Which the fire sends around on the hearth ;
    As the glasses we clink,
    Full of care-killing drink,
Let our toasts of true friendship arise ;
    This one night in the year,
    We can keep back the tear,
Which too often is found in our eyes.

    Oh ! I love the dear time
    That I sing in my rhyme,
When good will to all men should be found
    In our hearts and our brains,
    And be sung in our strains,
Till our voices in union resound.
    There is time for our care—
    For our grief and despair—
In the months rolling rapidly by,
    But to-night we must sing,
    Ere the moments take wing,
And away from our presence they fly.

PLEASURE AND PASTIME.

Thinks I, here's the month pretty near at an end,
    And how have I squander'd my time ?
I pledged myself, truly, this year I would send
    Every month to the *Journal*, a rhyme.

My subject? I don't know of what I shall write,
　But patience, dear reader, I'll try
And give you a confab, took place t'other night,
　Between my old mother and I.

The noble old dame, with her hair silvered o'er,
　Sat close by my side, at the fire,
The ground with the frost of December, was hoar,
　But stilled was the Storm King's ire.
Her eyes labored hard thro' the mists of the years,
　To read the Good Word, but in vain.
She laid down the book 'mid her fast falling tears,
　And thus, of old age did complain.

"Oh Shandy, my life-tide is ebbing away,
　The gloom gathers fast, and I feel
A dread of the dawn of eternity's day—
　That soon shall its terrors reveal.
A pilgrimage here on this earth I have made,
　Yet, life has had blessings for me.
But Shandy, acushla! I'm greatly afraid
　An orphan, you shortly will be."

"My mother," I said, as I kissed her dear brow;
　Touched lightly by sixty odd years,
"Cheer up, let my future not trouble you now,
　No need for your fast falling tears,

Because there's an old woman's daughter I know,
    Possessed of both beauty and grace,
Who fervently prays to the tomb you may go,
    Until she steps into your place."

God bless me! the change on her features that
        came,
    Was joyful, indeed, to behold;
Life kindled anew, and you'd say the dear dame
    Was neither decrepit nor old.
'Twas always my plan when she talked about
        death,
    To tell her, another was nigh
Who'd care for her son, she'd recover her breath,
    And the olden time glance of her eye.

My brothers—all you of the Benedict-clan—
    Whose wives are inclined to complain,
Who'll tell you they're dying, just follow my plan,
    Console them in just such a strain.
Yes tell them, as I told my mother that night;
    I'll wager my life all their aches,
Their pains, and their ailments, will quickly take
        flight,
    If not I will forfeit the stakes.

" Ah Shandy, you rascal, you'd wish I were dead
    And out of your sight in the grave."

"Oh no, my dear mother," I soothingly said,
  " 'Tis yourself about orphans did rave."
"But Shandy, confess, you've a wife in your
    eye."
  "Yes, mother, resplendent in charms,
And just in a month from the moment you die
  I'll have the dear girl in my arms."

"You rascal, I'll live to defeat all your plans,
  When the evening arrives you will see
Me step to the altar, forbidding the bans,
  No grandmother titles for me."
I kissed her good night, I vacated my seat,
  To meet with as jolly a crew
As ever tripped lightly, on musical feet,
  In the ball-room of "One-Fifty-Two."

Dear reader, in dreams have you ever been bless'd
  With views of those mansions of light,
Where souls, weary laden, find refuge and rest,
  In those realms of endless delight?
A counterpart here, on this earth you would find
  That night of our annual ball,
The sight would be always engraved on your mind
  Of splendor adorning our hall.

Flags, banners, and bunting, suspended in air,
  With mirrors—life-size—on the wall.

Choice paintings, selected with excellent care,
    Profusely adorning the hall.
And rare birds, whose melody swell'd on the night,
    In waves of voluptuous song,
With fountains that played in the chandelier's
    light,
    Admired by a beautiful throng.

The hours flew by on winged feet as we lanced
    To music's most ravishing thrill,
The minutes but seconds all seemed as we danced
    The schottische, the waltz, and quadrille.
Gray streaks in the east brought the night to a
    close,
    The moments too rapidly flew ;
A night that will ne'er be forgotten by those
    In the ball-room of " One-Fifty-Two."

I jumped into bed a short nap to secure,
    In prayers not a second did waste,
My eyes were just closed, when a voice at the door
    Said, " Shandy, your wanting in haste,
You're marked on the board, so be off with your
    train,"
    The caller exclaimed with a sneer.
And up from my heart that was surging in pain
    I cursed him in language sincere.

MY CASTLE IN SPAIN.

I've a castle near a wildwood,
   Trellised o'er with ivy green ;
Where I've often played in childhood,
   And in older years am seen.
There I go to sit and ponder,
   After many a toilsome hour,
Where my heart can throb the fonder,
   In a sun-lit dreamer's bower.

In this castle lives a maiden,
   True and tender as the dove;
One whose heart is over-laden
   With the purest kind of love.
She has sunny ringlets flowing,
   O'er her neck and shoulders, too,
And her lips are ripe and glowing,
   With the cherry's crimson hue.

I have gilded coaches rolling,
   On the gravelled walks around ;
Blooded steeds, which need controlling,
   As they restive paw the ground ;
But my grooms are skilled and daring,
   Every man within my train,
Who has brand new livery wearing,
   Loves my castle built in Spain.

There are trees, where birds, delighted,
   Sing in chorus loud and long ;
I can never say I'm slighted,
   For they give me joyous song.
I have fountains constant playing,
   In the sunlight on the lawn ;
And the breeze keeps hammocks swaying,
   Where my vassals sleep till dawn.

Mirth and music, fun and laughter,
   Ev'ry moment, all may hear ;
From the draw-bridge to the rafter,
   There is neither care nor fear ;
For each moment has its pleasure,
   And we many bumpers drain,
All flow o'er with honest measure,
   In my castle built in Spain.

1 have friends who sit beside me,
   All like brothers tried and true ;
They have ne'er been known to chide me,
   Nor reflect on what I do ;
In their eyes I read affection,
   All are sociably inclined,
Not a single imperfection
   Can be found in heart or mind.

I have coffers flowing over
    With the treasures of the land,
Where they are you'll soon discover,
    If you'll join my happy band.
I will lead you straight and willing
    In amongst the hoarded gain,
Where you'll find your bosom thrilling
    At my riches o'er in Spain.

'I am monarch of this castle,
    And I reign with royal power;
Not a liegeman nor a vassal
    But may have a prince's dower;
For I ne'er can miss my treasures,
    Tho' they millions take away,
Still they'll leave me flowing measures
    To distribute ev'ry day.

I have musty tomes of learning,
    Thoughts of men long dead and gone,
Where I hourly spend discerning
    What their brains were bent upon.
Ancient lore, where infant Science
    Struggles into life and day;
Written with a sure reliance
    That upon life's page 'twould stay.

There Religion, pure and holy,
  At her altars may be seen ;
Out amongst the meek and lowly
  Oft she strays with modest mien.
In her footsteps all may wander,
  For she leads to light divine,
To a castle builded yonder,
  Where the stars of glory shine.

I would like to stay for ever
  In its grand old massive halls,
Where the clouds of care come never,
  Nor a shade of trouble falls.
But, alas ! I cannot tarry,
  Save to give my weary brain
Time to rest from grievous worry,
  In my castle o'er in Spain.

AIR CASTLES.

Dear Kittie : Last night I was building
  A beautiful castle in Spain.
I sat ornamenting and gilding,
  Tormented with torturing pain.
A voice all around me kept ringing,
  Like musical peals from above,

Some fair one melodiously singing,
  Of compliments, kisses, and love.

My castle completed, I wandered
  O'er walks of bright, velvety green.
One brief little moment I pondered
  On who I'd select as my queen;
The very next moment I found her,
  As Cupid let quiver his dart,
And there on my bosom I crowned her,
  The queen of my castle and heart.

With feelings of exquisite pleasure,
  We dallied the evening along;
'Twas joy to my heart beyond measure,
  To hear her melodious in song.
With compliments, love, and sweet kisses,
  The moments too rapidly flew;
A pause in our melting caresses
  Soon told me my darling was you.

"Oh, Heaven!" I cried, "in thy power
  Send blessings, the choicest above,
To give to my queen in her bower,
  With compliments, kisses, and love.
I awoke suffocating with pleasure,
  The sun through my lattice did gleam,
And faded away was my treasure;
  Dear Kittie, 'twas only a dream.

MOLLIE'S WOOING.

The moon was just creeping up over the hill,
 As I strolled to the tryst where my lover
Was waiting. My heart with affection did thrill,
 The dear little maid to discover.
The nightingale's notes full of melody were,
The evening was balmy, the sweet summer air
Was laden with bloom of the hawthorne there,
 And essence of newly-cut clover.

I found her in tears, but I kissed them away,
 And both of our breaths were united;
I told her to hurry without more delay,
 Too long our affections were plighted.
I showed her the ring and I told her the priest
Was waiting with guests to partake of the feast,
I could see that her weeping quite suddenly ceased,
 And she nestled up closely, delighted.

She feared that her mother would never consent
 To her wedding a light-hearted rover;
"If you take her advice," I replied, "you'll repent,
 And, besides, you will lose a true lover."
"Then we'll marry, she said, "let us hasten away
Or my feelings will change if I longer delay."
It was thus I won Mollie, the frolicsome fay,
 Mid the perfume of newly-cut clover,

TO MISS EMMA AVERY.

Written after reading her lines on "The Engineer."

Miss Avery, pardon this freak of my Muse,
To-night she insists on me taking a cruise
All over the strings of my harp, for a chime,
To tickle your fancy, in shape of a rhyme;
Perhaps I am hasty in making my bow,
And likely to get myself into a row,
That is if you think I am making too free,
Then train all your guns for a broadside on me.

I cannot resist the temptation to write;
My goosequill is "down in the corner" to-night,
Since reading your lines so truly sincere
In praise of the poor, over-worked engineer.
Thinks I to myself " Arrah Shandy, avick,
That girl's a trump, and she's good for a trick,
No matter how poor be the cards she may hold,
There's one you can't purchase for blarney or gold.
You'll find it a heart, and may wager your life
That card will yet make her an engineer's wife."

God knows I have often repined at my lot,
When'er the old mill wasn't steaming and hot—
And this is the clime, and the time of the year,
To torture the heart of the poor engineer—
I've many times jumped from the seat in a rage,

And thrown my old hat at the face of the gauge ;
My right eye devoted to watching the track ;
The left one admiring the pointer trot back ;
With snowdrifts ahead, alongside, and behind ;
My nose of an indigo hue from the wind ;
When slipping, and sliding, and crawling along,
No prospect to cheer me, but everything wrong,
In midst of such dire desolation, my lot
Is sweetened to think we're not wholly forgot.
And, mind you, a great many times I could name
Of perilous moments which add to our fame ;
But what is the use ? I would rather by far
Have a seat by your side in a drawing-room car,
And whisper my gratitude into your ear,
As thanks for your lines on the poor engineer.

I hope you'll not think I have too much to do
By asking a short, little question of you, .
"Have you a young chap within glance of your
      eye ˙
Who throws you a kiss as he passes you by ;
Who makes you a movement—a wave of the
      hand ?
No matter, so long as you both understand."
Your answer to me will be "yes," I'll go bail
Your lover is some noble knight of the rail,
Who has earned his spurs, and will wear them
      forever,

By faithful attention to throttle and lever;
If not will you grant my most earnest desire,
Reflect, and become Mrs. Shandy Maguire?

How happy I'd feel on the railroad of life
If I had a girl like you for a wife.
I'd scorn all dangers, privations, and dread,
My heart would be light, not an ache in my head,
We'd live just as happy as birds in a cage,
Surrounded by offspring to bless our old age;
And, now, my dear friend, do not think me too
    bold
By saying you'd suit me, no matter how old.
I don't care a fig for a girl of sixteen,
No more than I love stealing apples when green;
With grapes 'tis the same, don't we prize them
    the most,
And find them delicious, when touched by the
    frost?
Don't think your admirer inclined to a joke
When saying—old pipes are the best for a smoke;
The wreathes from a dudeen are sweeter by far,
Than those from a meerschaum, or fragrant cigar;
Just so with a woman, with grapes, and my pipe,
She's always the sweetest when lusciously ripe;
These similes all may sound vulgar to you,
They're such as I have but you'll find they are
    true,

In behalf of the boys I return you my thanks,
I hope you will win a good prize from our ranks,
A brave-hearted, handsome, and dashing young
 gent,
Who'll ne'er give you cause of your choice to
 repent;
If such a young fellow you fail to procure,
Just drop me a line, and I'll answer you sure.
Who knows but together we'll yet have the road,
Assisting each other to carry life's load.

———

SHOW MERCY TO THE ERRING.

Show some mercy to the erring,
 Do not kick a brother down;
Let him feel your clasp fraternal,
 And conceal the cruel frown;
For his heart is only human,
 And temptation's very strong;
Had he but superior reason,
 He could guard against the-wrong.

If our hearts were all transparent,
 And exposed to other's view,
We might not be so determined
 Fallen brothers to pursue;

9

But while hid from observation
    Are our many vicious deeds,
We will swing the lash of torture
    On our victim 'till he bleeds.

I have heard "stop thief" resounding
    On the streets before to-day,
From the throats of cunning rascals,
    Who could hide their theft away;
While the luckless wretch who pilfer'd
    A much needed loaf of bread,
Was condemned before the people,
    And away to prison led.

If a sister errs she never
    Can regain the ground she lost;
And her heartless sex are ready
    To condemn her acts the most;
They will not reflect in pity
    On the ills she must endure,
But they scourge her with a vengeance,
    While her wronger is secure.

If we'd judge mankind in mercy,
    We would surely fill the plan,
That our Saviour from the Mountain
    Gave for government of man;

And perhaps He'd judge us kindly,
   When we'd stand before His throne,
For the mercy shown to others
   Will to us by Him be shown.

THE REPLY TO "A REQUEST" OF L. C. W.

Ah! here comes the *Journal*, 'tis promptly on
      time,
   Perusing its pages to me is a pleasure;
I eagerly gloat o'er each letter and rhyme,
   Regardless of purity, diction or measure.
Who cares for a lack of grammatical rules?
   They never were written by critics or scholars,
Who boast of the years they have slumbered in
      schools,
   Then value a man by his number of dollars.

What's here? Why a little request, as I live,
   I judge on perusal it comes from a brother.
Who, in a few lines, a tough subject can give,
   When making reply to the son of my mother.
I never could swallow historical lore,
   'Twas always considered a sign of good breed-
      ing
To sit with a few of the boys at the door,
   And mimic all those who were fond of such
      reading.

"Perhaps I'm a nobleman traveling incog,
   Who squandered my youth near the lakes of
     Killarney : ''
Perhaps at New York I have seen your phizog,
   And heard your sweet tongue running over
     with blarney.
In heraldry's books noble lineage I trace :
   I am one of the Macs, and will ever stand by
     her ;
Consigned to oblivion in shame and disgrace
   Be the renegade wretch who would basely deny
     her.

I fain would reply to your honest request,
   Provided my Muse was accomplished and
     ready ;
Of late she's indulging in indolent rest,
   And rather inclined to be prudish and steady.
And yet what a subject, 'tis worthy the pen
   Of learning's most noble and gifted of sages,
To sing of fair daughters and brave-hearted men
   That Erin can boast on her history's pages.

Each hill-top and valley adorning her land,
   Have witnessed the tide of her sons' crimson
     slaughter ;
Her passes had spartans, each brave-hearted
     band

Have struggled for freedom till blood ran like
    water.
And centuries hence, should the fight be prolonged,
    Her tyrants will find in her cause we grow
    braver,
Her martyrs on scaffolds declared she was
    wronged,
    When dying, their latest fond breath was "God
    save her."

In life's early years through her gem-spangled
    fields,
    I sported my happiest, sunniest hours,
Inhaling perfume that the sweet-brier yields,
    And weaving rich garlands of beautiful flowers.
Long years have elapsed since I parted her shores,
    And memory fails to recall early faces,
Yet, land of my birth, from my heart's richest
    stores,
    I send you an offspring's fond love and em-
    braces.

Though dear to my heart is the land of my birth,
    And worthy of true patriotic affection,
Yet, dearer Columbia, fair queen of the earth,
    That gives the oppressed of all nations protec-
    tion.

Oh, long may her banner float gloriously free,
  O'er millions of men in fraternal communion,
Proud emblem of freedom on land and on sea,
  All hail to the starry-gemmed flag of this Union.

———

BABY'S WELCOME.

Come, my baby, till I kiss you,
  On your flushy, frowsy face.
You will get a royal welcome
  To our humble little place.
We have waited for your coming
  With anxiety sincere,
But the Lord be thanked, my cherub,
  You are landed safely here.

'Tis a world bleak and cheerless,
  Which you've entered to reside,
But a heart both brave and fearless,
  Can enjoy its sunny side.
We will guard you late and early,
  Give you most devoted care,
'Till you're old enough to battle
  With its variable air.

Ah! your mother's eyes are beaming
  From beneath your tiny lids,
And they send me backward dreaming,
  Mongst the songs of Katydids ;
By the moonlight, in the valley,
  Where we rambled side by side,
On the evening when she promised
  To become my blooming bride.

Little stranger ! there is pleasure
  In recalling such a scene.
I would not exchange my treasure
  For the ransom of a queen.
You will find her true and tender
  And affectionate to thee ;
She'll be gentle and devoted,
  As she's always been to me.

When you're old enough to toddle
  With your dimpled hand in mine,
We will ramble out together,
  And I'll cull you flowers fine ;
We will listen to the warbling
  Of the birds upon the trees,
And amid the scented clover,
  We will chase the humming bees.

We've a cozy cot, to lull you
   Into quiet, peaceful rest;
And you're sure of healthy nurture
   From your mother's tender breast;
And we'll lavish on you kindness,
   And we'll fondle you with love,
For you look just like an angel
   Heaven sent us from above.

HOPE, THE DECEIVER.

There are moments when life does not seem worth
   possessing,
   When faint and exhausted we're glad to lie
   down;
When Miss Fortune, instead of donating a bless-
   ing,
   Repulses us off with a withering frown.

When we count on a share of her manifold treas-
   ures,
   The whimsical jade is uncertain and coy;
And she guards in a miserly manner her meas-
   ures,
   A portion of which we would gladly enjoy.

Many times I have tender'd unbounded affection,
And earnestly sued for a smile in exchange ;
But I never yet got her false heart in subjection,
Although I have tried till my brains I'd de-
range.

She is like a young maiden, light-hearted and
fickle,
Who boasts of her conquests, still seeking for
more—
Like a fair one who oft kept my heart in a pickle—
The same as she did many others before.

But for Hope, the deceiver, in language uncivil,
I'd rail at her hourly, for days that are gone,
When she treated me worse than her kinsman,
the Devil,
E'en now she deludingly beckons me on.

I will follow once more and perhaps my devotion
May meet from the damsel a fitting reward ;
Who can tell but at last she has taken the notion,
To change into smiles all the tears of the bard ?

TO THE ROBIN RED-BREAST.

Hear the robin red-breast full of harmony trill,
As he gathers the crumbs which I placed on the
    sill.
For his simple repast he repays me in song,
Which he pours from his throat in glad numbers
    along.
He is joyous, domestic, and free from all care ;
He will hop to within a few feet of my chair ;
He is fearless, because of the kindness he's shown,
And 'tis seldom he leaves me to ponder alone.

Little red-breasted warbler, you've found out the
    art,
Which your instinct has taught you will reach to
    my heart ;
For each note strikes a chord of affection, whose
    tone
Will respond to no touch but of music alone ;
And your melody bubbles in fountains so bright,
That I gladly enjoy every song with delight,
And I feel full of praise for the gifts you bestow,
With your sense-charming song in the sun's
    golden glow.

'Mongst the denizens winging their way through
    the air,
Oh, I prize you the dearest of all that are there ;

For tradition relates at the cross you were found,
When the blood of the Saviour flowed to the
    ground,
And in pity your breast you plunged into the tide,
Where it crimsoned your plumage on Calvary's
    side.
Full of gentleness ever, dear songster, you'll be,
And you'll always be welcome, sweet warbler, to
    me.

  .

TO MRS. E. M. HOOKER.

DEAR MADAM :
Since first I was kicked through the portals of life,
    To battle my way in oppression and pain,
When seeking subsistence in warfare and strife,
    With naught to assist me but muscle and brain,
I've met with far more than my share of the ills
That are known to us all as " mortality's pills, "
I have seen the cold glance of ineffable scorn,
Flung into my face since the hour I was born,
And many times, madam, I've fallen by the way,
Discouraged, down-hearted, depressed with the
    fray.
The good I have done as I journey'd along,
Was always pronounced inexcusably wrong ;

Suspicion surrounds me, and you 'mongst the
    rest,
  Accuse me of chasing the bauble of fame;
Dear madam, I hope you were really in jest,
    When thinking me guilty of changing my name.

What object, in Heaven's name, had you in view,
    To call me so plainly, " a wonderful lyre ? "
I'm really surprised at a lady like you,
For doubting my name to be Shandy Maguire. •
That noble old name down the ages has run,
Bequeathed by the father to honor the son;
I peer through the gloom of the years, and I trace
A noble, a princely, a chivalrous race,
Their swords from their sheathes ever ready to
    draw,
When fighting for justice and scorning the law;
The fat of the land they would always procure,
And pass it around through the lean of the poor;
But, madam, alas, what a change from the past;
The sky of the noble Maguires is o'ercast
With ominous clouds, this degenerate time,
When one of the family figures in rhyme.
Tormented by you, and some others whose game
Is telling the public I don't know my name;
Your questions were asked me so often before,
They grieved my poor heart till it bled at the core.

I've many times ran to the mirror, to stare,
And see if I really and truly stood there ;
Now madam, I'll furnish you proof from a dame,
   Who'll quickly convince you her son is no lyre,
And neither afraid nor ashamed of the name,
   That many suspect isn't Shandy Maguire.

"Dear mother"—I always address her as "dear,"
   "What is it my son ?" she replied with a laugh—
" Oh, something surprising, I'll sing in your ear,
   And mother, don't think I am tipping you
      chaff."
Now madam, I'm skillfully versed in the art
Of working my way to an old woman's heart,
With young ones, alas ! there's a difference there,
I might just as well whistle jigs to a bear,
As make a young woman believe what I say,
When talking of love in a neighborly way.
A certain young lady, for five years at least,
I'm asking to let me go talk to the priest,
Her only replies are "be patient and cool,
Don't bother me, Shandy, you act like a fool."
I sometimes believe she is heartless and cold,
Perhaps I'll succeed when the darling grows old.

But back to my subject : "Dear mother, my mind
Is sorely distracted, no peace can I find ;

I'm bothered, tormented, derided in scorn,
I wish in my heart I had never been born."
A moment I paused, to recover my breath,
My mother, she seem'd in the stupor of death,
She knew every word I expressed was the truth,
I never was caught telling lies in my youth;
Whenever I chanced of an evening to roam,
She'd ask in the morning, the time I came home,
I'd tell her the truth, she would say she was sure
I didn't make much of a fuss at the door;
I didn't indeed; she'd be snoring asleep,
As in through a window I'd cautiously creep,
My boots in my pockets, to guard against noise,
When having a game of " Ould Sledge " with the
    boys.
I slept with my brother, an urchin called Mick,
And he was the rooster could tumble and kick.
His feet at an angle of ninety degrees
Would fly in a tangent away from his knees;
He'd hurl me out of the bed, in his might,
To dream on the floor all the rest of the night.
I dare not complain, as that boy was no fool,
Altho' he ne'er saw the inside of a school.
He'd rifle my pockets of Killikinnick,
He'd smoke my old pipe till his stomach grew
    sick,
He'd make me divide all the pennies I'd win,

To keep him from telling the way I got in.
Again I am off in what seems but a dream,
   A dear, happy dream of my juvenile years;
Now madam, I'm back to yourself and my theme;
   Spun out till the close amid fast falling tears.

"Dear mother, come gaze on me, straight in the
     eye,
   And answer my questions, don't think me in
     fun,
Please give me a candid and truthful reply,
   For Heaven's sake tell me if I am your son?
Are you my old mother? be sure you are right,
Does Shandy Maguire stand before you to-night?
Or is it some other spalpeen in his place,
Who's bringing the family name to disgrace?
Sometimes in the South I'm advancing a claim,
And beating the boys on the strength of my name,
Again, in the West, in a round-house I'm seen,
Soliciting alms in a manner that's mean,
Right here, at my home I find little relief,
The story flies round, I'm a pilfering thief;
Such rumors are really injurious, because
The Lord only knows where the villains will
     pause;
I wouldn't at all be surprised if I'd hear
The sheriff was playing with hemp at my ear,

And sending me off from the troubles of life
For running away with another man's wife.
Or some such a mean, inexcusable crime,
Bad luck to the day I first jingled a rhyme ;
Since then I can date many ills, for I swear,
I'm troubled just now with far more than my
    share.
'Oh, what's in a name?' said a moonshiny youth,
  Whose course of true love wasn't steered among
    flowers,
I really can't tell about his, but in truth,
Dear mother, I think there's the devil in ours."

Like a sprig of sixteen, the old girl arose,
  Her knitting unconsciously fell from her hand,
Her spectacles dropped from her eyes to her nose,
  And there in amazement before me did stand.
"Poor boy," were the words she expressed,"what
  a loon ;
You're always deranged at the full of the moon."
" There are two of us so," I replied ; then her eye
  Suggested a hint from her reach to retire.
My very next chance, I'll embrace it and try
  To prove to you, madam, I'm Shandy Maguire.

LOSS OF THE SCHOONER ".PERSIAN," ON LAKE HURON.

Sad and dismal is the tale,
    Which I'll relate to you,
About the schooner Persian,
    Her officers and crew,
Who sank beneath the stormy deep,
    To rise in life no more ;
Where winds with desolation sweep,
    Lake Huron's rock-bound shore.

They left Chicago on their lee,
    Their singing did resound ;
All hearts were full of joyous glee,
    As homeward they were bound ;
They little thought the monster, Death,
    Was lurking in the deep,
And they, so full of life and hope,
    Should in the waters sleep.

In mystery their doom is sealed,
    They did collide some say,
And that is all will be revealed
    Until the judgment day ;
When the angel takes his stand,
    To 'wake the waters blue,
And summon forth,by heaven's command,
    The ill-starr'd Persian's crew.

10

No mother's hand was there to press
    The brow's distracting pain ;
No gentle wife, with kind caress,
    To soothe the aching brain ;
No lover there, no sister nigh,
    Nor little ones to weep ;
In wat'ry graves henceforth they'll lie,
    Beneath the stormy deep.

Her gallant captain is no more,
    He fills a seaman's grave ;
Beneath the deep, off Huron's shore,
    Where wind-tossed waters rave ;
Unknown the spot, and hid from view
    His manly, lifeless form ;
And stilled in death the tar so true,
    Who weathered many a storm.

Daniel Sullivan, her mate,
    A tar as bold and brave,
As ever was compelled by fate,
    To fill a sailor's grave ;
He will be weeped for as a friend,
    Alas ! his days are o'er,
He met a sad, untimely end,
    Near Huron's rock-bound shore,

Oh, Dan, your many friends will mourn
    That fate did on you frown;
We'll look in vain for your return,
    To your adopted town;
We'll miss the love-glance of your eye,
    Your hand we'll press no more,
For stilled in death, old friend, you lie
    Near Huron's rock-bound shore.

Her sailors' names we did not know,
    Excepting one or two;
Down in the deep they all did go,
    They were a luckless crew.
Oh, not a man escaped to land.
    To clear the mystery o'er,
Until they drift, by heaven's command,
    In lifeless form ashore.

Around Presque-Isle, the sea-birds scream
    In mournful notes along;
They're chaunting forth the requiem,
    The dismal funeral song;
They skim along the waters blue,
    And then aloft they soar,
In memory of the Persian's crew,
    Near Huron's stormy shore.

TO " MOBILIAN."

"Mobilian," all the dreamy past,
In fond array, each friendly face
That 'round me in those days were cast
Your lines recalled.   I love to trace
The scenes at eve where oft I've strayed;
The myrtle bower, the silent glade,
The star gemm'd sky of deepest blue;
The walk where lovers went to woo,
The balmy waves of rich perfume,
From orange groves where all was bloom;
The nightingale's sweet plaintive song,
By zephyrs borne swift along,
Until the atmosphere around
Gave echo to the charming sound;
The bay, its shores, the grove, the hill,
Are all enshrined in mem'ry still
And stereotyped upon my heart.
   Your lines awoke the dreamy whole—
They moved by panoramic art
   Through silent mansions of my soul.

When groping through the gloom of years,
   When toiling on in grief and pain,
With scarcely time to chase the tears
   That dim the eye and flood the brain,
We seldom backward turn to view

Those scenes that wear a roseate hue ;
Scenes, with a retrospective eye,
We trace, amid those days gone by,
Where, heart entwined in heart, the twain
Have lived, and feared not future pain,
Until the parting moment drove
Them far away from scenes of love.
Your lines awoke a plaintive thrill
That haunts the halls of mem'ry still,
And I, my friend, to-night would fain
Prolong the melancholy strain,
But ruder scenes of toil and strife
    Command me hence.   "Mobilian" dear,
Where'er my lot be cast in life,
    I'll always keep your precepts near.

FATHER MATHEW TEMPERANCE SOCIETY.

OSWEGO, N. Y.—TENTH ANNIVERSARY, 1878.

Old mother, a decade of years have sped on
    Since I, a poor waif, weather-beat by the storm,
Approached you to take the proud title of "son,"
    And muster myself in your ranks of reform.
At annual feasting I've always been here,
To read you a song and partake of your cheer ;
To-night by the laws of both custom and love,

I come, as of yore, my affection to prove;
And till but one drop of my life-tide remains—
Till it stops at my heart and congeals in my veins,
In joy, or in sorrow, in mirth, or despair,
In tempest, or sunshine, foul weather or fair,
The years shall still find me as onward they glide,
In person or spirit right here at your side;
I speak from experience, my words bear their
    weight,
    Through waves of temptation I've passed and
      proved true,
I've yielded obedience both early and late
    To all the wise rules promulgated by you.

So much for myself, now, my noble, old dear,
    I'll on with my task without further delay;
Please grant me a moment or two at your ear,
    To talk of affairs in a family way.
Bethink you the time when you first settled down
And made your abode in this tax-ridden town,
With looks of suspicion your coming was chilled,
But soon our old homestead grew gloriously
    filled;
In here came the husbands when led by their
    wives,
And pledged to live sober the rest of their lives.
So times sped along and our numbers increased,

And guest followed guest to partake of the feast,
With song, and with chorus, in mirth and good
   cheer,
We drifted away from rum, whiskey and beer.
We sat here for hours meditating on rules ;
   Lawmakers were scarce in our midst, but a few
Spruce, dignified Solomons, fresh from the schools,
   Supposed they could act as it pleased them to do.

But, mother, acushla ! we loved you too well,
   We sprang to our *posts* and we shortened their
      sails,
We made a short job of each long-talking swell,
   By shaking a small grain of salt on their *tales*.
Temptation crept in and dissensions grew rife,
They threatened, alas ! to deprive you of life ;
But, darling ! you live, you survived ev'ry shock,
We soon drove the black-sheep away from the
   flock.
To those who were honest and truly sincere,
We always rewarded their efforts in here ;
And honored them well, as our records will show,
With every good gift in our power to bestow.
To those who proved traitors and fell by the way,
Alas ! who can tell where they're scattered to-
   day ?
Some lie in their graves and some live to complain,

And curse their misfortune for drinking again.

Many more, and I'm sure that their numbers
are scores,

They sought an excuse to escape through our
doors.

You saved them, and then they denied you sup-
port,

They scamper'd away to some other resort.

Like birds when full-fledged, they deserted the
nest,

And they sought other scenes, well, perhaps they
done best.

You've more, your young grandsons, who think
they are wise,

They wish you to look more refined in their eyes ;

They scoff at their father's good counsels, and say

Their granny they'll deck out in fashion's array,

They'll "re-organize you," whatever that means,

I see by the droll-looking glance of your eye,

You'll never elope with those gents in their teens,

Who'd quickly desert you and leave you to die.

Dear mother, now banish all troublesome fears,

Your first-born sons have been ever the same,

They've guided you on o'er the pitfalls of years,

And here by your side they will add to your
fame,

Let old Time roll along, let the years pass us by,

We have strength to protect you, our foes we'll
    defy.
There is peace here and plenty for those who can
    shun,
The deadliest poison known under the sun.
Moral suasion's the weapon we always employ,
When we meet with the foe that our lives would
    destroy ;
Prohibition may do for those slow moving bands,
Who invoke legislature to strengthen their
    hands.
Our success won your smiles for a decade of years.
    We are robust and hearty to-night, my old
      dame,
And our features are wreathed with smiles,'stead
    of tears,
    Which we'll wear evermore if we honor your
      name.

TO THE AUTHOR OF " SUNDAY LABOR."

You ask what I think of this Sabbath-day work,
    Or if there is cause to complain,
When a man is denounced as a " good-for-naught
    shirk"·
    For refusing to go with his train ?
Your questions I'll answer as well as I can

With all the respect that is due
To one of your sex, from a kind-hearted man
    Who'd kneel and pay homage to you.

By jove! I am truly in love with your pen!
    Your Muse is defiantly bold,
Such women as you are worth more to their men,
    Than their weight of the dross we call gold.
If you have a sister, unmarried, I swear
    I'd like the dear creature to woo!
There's nothing would brighten my prospects
        more fair
    Than a chance to claim kindred with you.

With Sabbath-day work we're not troubled much
        here,
    We thank Mr. Phelps and Sam Sloan;
They give us those fifty-two days every year
    For sins of the week to atone.
On Sabbath-day running that's all I can say,
    Because I'm not "pinched by the shoe,"
But, madam, hereafter on Sunday I'll pray
    For God to have pity on you.

Now, madam, draw near, I will whisper a plan,
    Should the like ever happen again,—
You'll find it will aid and assist the "old man,"
    If he don't want to go with the train.

Don't have any fear for him losing his job,
 Providing you'll faithfully do
Your part, with a truly affectionate throb
 Of wifely devotion in you.

Those engine despatchers are hard chaps to fool,
 They doubt every mournful tale.
But madam, I'll give you a short, simple rule—
 I have never yet known it to fail :
He then can respond to a call with a will,
 Providing your part you will do
The engine despatcher will see he is ill,
 And back he will send him to you.

Rub the poor fellow's tongue with a morsel of
  chalk,
 'Twill make it look sickly and white ;
Hit the 'tickle-bone' in his left elbow a knock ;
 His pulse any doctor will fright;
Then, tell him his mother-in-law got a fall,
 And died from effects of it too.
His features will blanch, and his look will appal
 The engine despatcher, and you.

Clasp hands across States, this acquaintance
  begun
 'Twixt you and myself must not end.
And, madam, I tell you, devoid of all fun,

I'm proud to be classed as your friend.
Write on for the edification of those
   Who hazardous labor pursue,
Pour in your hot shot to the camps of our foes,
   And soon they'll strike colors to you.

WHERE DO THE WICKED SLEEP?

"Where do the wicked sleep, sexton, come tell?
Where in your gloomy domain do they dwell?
Are they apart from the true and the just?
Here are their bones left to mingle in dust?
Point out their graves so I'll trample in scorn
Over them, fiends from the hour they were born.
Where are they hidden? No name can I trace;
Only the just are interred in this place.

Epitaphs telling of brave men and true,
Chiselled in marble, exposed to my view;
Virtues abundant lie under the ground,
None but the upright of earth have I found.
Surely you know where the wicked are laid,
Here where you hid them, with mattock and
    spade;
Sexton, its bearings, pray have you forgot?
Where do the wicked sleep? point out the spot.

Here mausoleums and obelisks tell
Only where virtue and righteousness dwell.
Think you the wicked could peacefully rest
Here in such holiness, here 'mid the blest?
Monuments grandly on all sides arise,
Telling of pure angels called to the skies.
Sexton, for decades you've wielded the hoe,
Where do the wicked sleep? surely you know."

"Thirty long years have I wrought in this soil,
Thousands were brought who required my toil;
Never came one but was deeply deplored,
All had been called to reside with the Lord.
Stranger, you know what the proverb has said :
'Speak only good when you mention the dead.'
Judging by words which I heard at each bier,
Only the just have I buried in here.

"Seek you elsewhere, but I fear you will fail.
Human decisions don't always prevail.
Judgments erroneous from mankind depart.
No one yet fathomed the depths of the heart.
Springs there lie hidden, unknown, unexplored,
Sealed to the vision of all but the Lord.
He, from his throne with an allseeing eye,
Only can tell where the wicked ones lie,"

"ONLY A TRAMP."

" He's only a tramp," said the papers,
　　When telling the news of the day,
Of how a poor man was discovered,
　　Just breathing his last by the way.
And that was the epitaph written ;
　　And scarcely his spirit had fled,
When many around him had gathered,
　　To morbidly gaze on the dead.

Messieurs, let us pause and consider,
　　Right here o'er his mortal remains ;
A clue we, perchance, may discover,
　　'Twill be a reward for our pains.
From whence had he come, and bound whither,
　　His birth-place, and name to denote ;
What's this ? Ah ! Messieurs, 'tis a letter
　　Concealed in the breast of his coat.

We'll read : " My dear husband, this letter
　　I write to you, hoping 'twill be
Another strong link in love's fetter,
　　Which binds you so closely to me ;
My heart's dearest throbs of affection
　　I send to you, darling, and pray
Kind Heaven, for health and protection,
　　And speedy success on your way."

" Our children are silently sleeping ;
    I many times kiss them for you ;
But Freddie is ailing from weeping,
    And baby is troublesome too.
Yet cheerfully, darling, I labor
    'Till you some employment secure,
I'm helped by a kind-hearted neighbor,
    Who feels for the friendless and poor."

" This morning our Jennie ran sprightly,
    To kiss me, she whispered me : ' ma,
Kind angels converse with me nightly,
    And give me good tidings of pa.'
God favor our little romancer
    With virtuous dreams all her life.
Impatiently 'waiting your answer,
    Your faithful, affectionate wife."

Then silently stood each spectator ;
    Their eyes were o'erflowing with tears ;
Their lips—where the name of Creator,
    Had never been mentioned for years—
Were now breathing prayers full of pity
    To God, with an earnest desire
For those in a far distant city,
    Deprived of a husband and sire,

The tale can be told by that letter,
    Denied all employment at home,
His wretched condition to better,
    Away o'er the land he did roam.
Repulsed by continued denials,
    He came to seek rest on this sod,
At last there's an end to his trials,
    He rests with a merciful God!

And "only a tramp" said the papers,
    When telling the news of the day,
Of how that poor man was discovered
    Just breathing his last by the way;
That was the brief epitaph written;
    But scarcely the letter was read
Till many Samaritans gathered,
    To tenderly care for the dead.

TO DOCTOR REYNOLDS.

Dear Doctor, long I've thought your Muse was
    dead,
With laurel wreathed 'round her honored head;
But when your poem, written for the *Times*,
Came duly to me with its silvery chimes,
I learned, then, there was no cause for weeping,
Because the dame has not been dead, but sleeping.

My worthy friend, your grand, heroic strain,
Recalls the battle scenes of strife again,
And by the genius of your gifted pen,
You've lauded Hancock as the prince of men,
And urged your hero to the foremost place,
To make him win the Presidential race.
Your honest purpose, I, for one, admire,
But vain the labor of your gifted lyre ;
While Tilden lives, and he aspires to run,
You might as well fire off a " quaker " gun
As broadsides such as you're discharging here,
For Doctor, Tilden has the race-course clear.

My brother bard—I will such kinship claim—
Altho' my Muse is yet unknown to fame,
While yours may hover in sublimest flights,
And soar around the grand Olympic heights,
Mine, poor and lowly, in her native sphere
Is recognized on some occasions here.
I now suggest a short co-partnership,
'Twixt you and I upon a rhyming trip ;
We're sure to make a good, successful cruise,
And either one must own the lucky Muse.
Here are my plans : You must let Hancock slide,
He cannot stem the fierce politic tide ;
Then chorus up for Grant, I will for Tilden sing,
They both are centers of each inner ring.

11

If Grant should win we'll have the Empire sure,
And then, old friend, you can repose secure.
Sir Lawrence Reynolds you are sure to be,
Besides, a bone you oft can throw to me.
When plenty loads your noble tables down
In days when he will wear the kingly crown.

If Tilden wins, then by the Lord, I swear,
I'll give you, Doctor, sure, the lion's share!
I'll grind him rhymes out at a railroad pace,
And labor hard until he wins the race;
Then dine and feast you like a brother true
On dishes very seldom touched by you,
Provided, Doctor, you a cook do know,
Who understands the making hash from crow.

THE RHYMER TO HIS PEN.

Come here, my old pen, till we ramble along,
In the regions of fancy and the realms of song.
Disentangle the rushing, tumultuous throng
    Of thought-mazes, wild in my brain.
Now down in the ink, and my subject will be
Whatever runs freely, beneath this green tree;
If you prompt it in scorn or chorus in glee,
    I'll gladly prolong the refrain.

You've many times suffered your share of abuse,
Since plucked from the wing of Peg Flaherty's
    goose,
Because, my old friend, you have failed to produce
        A smile on the features of all.
But, know you, the numerous critical pack,
Who rush in their ire to encumber our track,
May suffer the torture of thumbscrew or rack,
        If on them with vengeance you fall.

True sportsmen have never perverted their aim
By firing at fowl not regarded as game,
And you, my companion, must do just the same,
        Regardless of ignorant fools,
Who seek to deride every stanza you sing;
And, like an assassin, their implements fling,
To silence your strain with their envious sting;
        We scorn all their laws and their rules.

The Lord in His majesty wisely designed
A wonderful mixture to make of mankind;
Oh, many he dwarfed both in person and mind,
        And spread them abroad o'er the earth.
Each movement and gesture, each action and
    shape,
Resembles entirely their grandfather ape,
You'd think from some jungle they made their
    escape—
        But Darwin accounts for their birth.

What stench-pools of filthy corruption there lie
Concealed in the hearts of the villains who try
To seek after slander, and then magnify
      The few simple words which they hear
A hundred fold more than the facts may disclose,
And then, with their eyes hanging down on each
    nose,
They'll run with the stuff to our deadliest foes,
      And pour their foul tales in each ear.

Some women are first to discover a trail,
And slander a sister, denounce her as frail;
Their bitter opinions they'll add to the tale,
      Wherein if we only could see
Such saints, when Temptation is hovering near,
And pouring a passionate plea in each ear;
Methinks they would merit their share of the
    sneer
      They throw 'round derisively free.

But some are well versed in the art to conceal
The treacherous moments from virtue they steal,
And those are the ones who unscabbard the steel,
      To cut with Satanical ire
The heart of a sister who falls by the way,
Forgetting, meanwhile, their dear selves are but
    clay,
But poor human nature, too prone to obey
      The beck of each tempting desire.

"Old Pen! we are often obliged to endure
The taunts which are flung at the friendless and
    poor,
By those who to-day are in sunshine secure,
        To-morrow the clouds may arise ;
If so, we will note them on life's rugged road,
To see how they'll carry adversity's load,
Methinks they will quiver when pricked by the
    goad,
        And sigh after sunnier skies."

———

TO THE CENTENNIAL COMMITTEE OF ONE HUNDRED.

Messieurs, 'tis a whimsical turn
    Of fancy that prompts me to write,
But fires patrioticly burn
    Deep down in my bosom to-night ;
And up from my heart comes a chorus—
    A clear, ringing, chorusing cheer,
When thinking of pleasure before us
    This joyous Centennial year.

In you, then, my honored committee,
    We place the full power to employ
A plan to enliven our city
    Three days in the month of July.

The programme already suggested
  Is excellent, sirs, in its way,
And I, by the boys am requested,
  A word on the subject to say:

We've twenty-one towns in this county,
  All peopled with patriots true,
Who'll come to partake of our bounty
  And see what we city-folk do.
From now until then they'll keep scanning
  The papers and programmes, to see
The plans the Committee are planning
  For this, our Centennial spree.

Announce in large letters each wonder
  We have from all parts of the earth,
Let cannon belch forth in loud thunder
  The dawn of the century's birth.
Send broadsides of congratulations
  To neighboring States, and proclaim
Abroad—to remotest of nations—
  Our love for great Washington's name.

Don't brood o'er next charter election,
  Or questions therewith to arise,
Because there's a little objection
  To some of us drawing a prize.

Besides, in political breakers
    The most skillful pilots we've found,
When steering amongst the slate-makers,
    We're run high and dry on the ground.

Now sirs, get your programmes in order,
    And scatter them broadcast; be sure
That plenty goes over the border,
    Our neighbor's from thence to secure.
Expense do not spare advertising,
    The sights which await them in store,
Historical, novel, surprising,
    When once they set foot on our shore.

Let nothing abridge our enjoyment,
    Let pleasure, for once, have full sway,
We'll all have some other employment,
    A century hence from to-day.
The reservoirs south of our city,
    With little expense can be made
Thirst quenchers, my honored Committee,
    And flow through our streets lemonade.

Such actions will pass down the ages,
    Surviving the shock of old Time;
Each name upon history's pages,
    Will loom in the future sublime.

One hundred years hence, what a story
  Each sire will relate to his son,
Of deeds full of honor and glory,
  Their noble old forefather's done !

Let each take his share of the labor,
  And not from his duty refrain ;
Who shirks off his part on his neighbor
  May hear from my bardship again.
My pen, I can scarcely control it,
  It's favorite theme is abuse,
Just because I unwittingly stole it
  Last week, from an Alderman's goose.

Remember, we're first among nations
  Existing to-day on the earth ;
Now work, sirs, and make preparations
  To greet such a century's birth.
This may be our last time together
  On such an occasion ; I fear
Will meet with a spell of hot weather,
  Before next Centennial year !

TO MADAM REBECCA.

(A REPLY TO HER ARTICLE HEADED "SHANDY MAGUIRE REVIEWED.")

Oh! Madam Rebecca—Dear Madam, I mean—
  My heart is o'erflowing with rapturous pleasure
Because in your loving review I have seen
  The objects I sought for, my long wished for
    treasure.
I've courted old women through life by the score,
Made love to the widows—a dozen or more;
I've sat with old maids till I thought I could spy
A faint little " yes " in each man-hunting eye;
I've sighed till I'm certain I saw in the air,
Fading off from my lips the grim ghost of despair,
As awkwardly sitting I'd gnaw my caubeen,
To shun the keen glance of a maid of sixteen.
But, all in their turn refused me so cool,
They caused me to think I was really a fool.
I next in the *Journal* fished round for a mate,
And, save a few nibbles, untouched lay the bait,
Till you, my own treasure and long sought for
    dove,
Sent deep in my heart the first spark of true love.
It was smoke all the others created, but you
Have set me in flame with your loving review.
I'd read it, then pause, and I'd read it again,
At home, in the roundhouse, or running my train;
I'd gloat o'er the lines with an eager delight,

And, Madam, I swear—though the act you'll
   be scorning—
I took that review into bed t'other night
   To clasp it up close in my bosom till morning.

Next dawn from a couch of sweet dreams I arose!
   Bewildered, delighted, like many another.
I scarcely took time to get into my clothes,
   Till off on Love's pinions I flew to my mother.
I showed her the *Journal*, I read your review,
I told her a wife I discovered in you.
I then, rich in fancy, enlarged on your charms,
And said I would soon have you clasped in my
   arms.
" Dear mother, I know she is comely and fair,
In natural curls I fancy her hair;
Her eyes must be bright—can out rival the stars,
My schoolmaster said were called Venus and
   Mars!
Her lips, like the cherries on Fogarty's tree!
So tempting of yore to an urchin like me;
Her teeth, a whole mouthful of pearls, and white
As new fallen snow in the sun's dawning light;
Her lips, I imagine, dear mother of mine,
Look just like a lily when smothered in wine?
Her arms are just what I need when we're wed
To serve me for pillows each night for my head.
Her bust, and her fair incomparable mien,

Will be a fit shrine for a husband's devotion;
And, mother, I'll cling to that beautiful queen
  Till summoned to cross over Time's troubled
    ocean.
" Oh, Shandy! my first-born, beautiful one!
  I pity your case and I'll try and console you;
For proving through life a good, dutiful son,
  I'll not let this Madam Rebecca, cajole you.
'Tis plain to be seen you're bewitched, I can trace
The spell of the siren o'erclouding your face.
You love-stricken fool, what a picture you draw
To gain my consent for a daughter-in-law.
Wherein, like myself, she is wrinkled and gray,
One eye artificial, her bones in decay;
Her curls clipped off from some poor girl's head;
Or may be her hair is a carroty red;
Her teeth are not pearls, but bones, far between,
Like milestones, with colorless lips for a screen;
Her bust and her waist are both padded and filled;
Besides, like yourself, at a rhyme she is skilled.
In the April number she struck up a tune,
Like the bay of a dog at a mid-winter moon,
I'll read you this extract, your passion 'twill kill;
A sample she ground in her doggerel mill:—

    " Then 'tis wheeze and cough and chow chow,
    Now puff and blow and pow pow.
    Back a jerk, forward a jump,

Couple to and then a bump,
A turn of the wheels, a scuff and clatter,
A shriek of the whistle, quadrupeds scatter,
The train moves forward, patter, patter.''
My son, she put that on the point of the dart,
That cupid let drive at your bachelor heart.
'Tis a sweet little song, can you give it an air,
And rattle it off on the strings of your lyre?
Troth, Shandy, you'll both make a musical pair,
If e'er she'll be Madam Rebecca Maguire!

Oh madam! 'Tis plain to be seen the old dame
Will never permit both our life-tides to mingle;
But, dearest! I swear by my love's glowing flame,
If you but consent I'll no longer live single.
I'll act disobediently once in my life,
'Tis I—not my mother—who's seeking a wife.
And, mind you, my idolized, musical dame,
'Tis just as you say about changing my name.
If Shandy don't suit you then Handy will do;
Most anything, darling! that's pleasing to you,
Because I'm determined together we'll run.
I don't care a pipe full of F. G. tobacco,
For all my old mother just preached to her son,
Providing you're satisfied, Madam Rebecca.

LINES WRITTEN AT THE REQUEST OF A WIDOWED FRIEND.

Dear Paddy, friend and brother,
　And companion of my youth,
Alas ! you're now a widower,
　I pity you in truth.
A wave of kind compassion
　Is sweeping o'r my soul
When thinking, darling Paddy,
　Of the grief you can't control.

Oh, yes, you'll weep in sadness
　For the " dear departed dove,
Now soaring with the angels,
　'Round the throne of God above."
By heaven ! there are thousands,
　Yes and tens of thousands, too,
Who'd weep one eye in darkness,
　To be free to-night like you !

I know your "darling Kittie,"
　Was a true and faithful wife,
More faithful than the husband
　She was wedded to in life.
I also know, dear Paddy,
　(And I'll keep the fact in view)
How the "darling dear departed,"
　Once did "mitten" me for you.

My boy ! I will console you
  With an epicedian strain,
I am at it now, dear Paddy,
  I am tortured with the pain !
I'll send it to the *Journal*,
  With the letter I've received,
So thirty thousand readers
  Can behold how much I'm grieved.

" In tears you will lament her,
  Till the gracious King above,
Will send for you to join her,
  In that home of peace and love !"
Now, Paddy, let me tell you,
  (And to this you will agree,)
If you're received in Heaven,
  There's a chance for such as me."

You must scourge your wicked body,
  Yes, and holy-stone your soul,
Before you can pass muster,
  At the call of Heaven's roll ;
It is hard to fool St. Peter,
  There's a duplex system there,
And all must have a ticket,
  Who would climb the golden stair !

Dear Paddy, list a moment,
  Do not let your passion rise,
When I tell you : not a blubber
  From your heart ran to your eyes ;
You may have squeezed a moisture,
  Like that monster of the Nile,
We all have read of, Paddy,
  Called "the weeping crocodile !"

You mention in your letter
  How you'll live for Kittie's sake,
A sad and lonely widower,
  No other bride you'll take;
You'll woo no other woman,
  Till your life-tide ebbs away—
"*The divil thrust you, darlint!*"
  As my country-women say.

I'll wager my existence,
  That before she's dead a year,
You'll be promenading, Paddy,
  With your hat hung on your ear ;
You'll be hunting up another,
  And a fox as old as you
Must have a tender chicken,
  My old sport, you're forty-two !

In justice to dear Kittie,
  With a tender, heartfelt sigh,
For days long fled forever,
  In happy times gone by,
I'll pen you here an epitaph—
  She earned it well in life,
And very few deserve it—
  "Here lies a faithful wife."

Take one advice I give you:
  Keep mute as mute can be,
Don't breathe a word in anger
  For singing thus to thee,
Because—and here I swear it—
  If you make the slightest noise,
I'll sing your name and number
  Next month for all the boys.

THE JOYS OF LABOR.

I hate to hear the clap-trap cry,
  Ascend at every grand ovation,
Until it reaches to the sky,
  From every toady in the nation—
How labor is a God-sent gift,
  And labor's sons we love as brothers,
Who, by their manly toil and thrift,
  Do honor to their noble mothers.

Messieurs, ye gem-bespangled throng,
    Whose tongues are with the blarney coated,
'Tis you who well may sing that song
    At banquets, where choice wine is noted;
Then spread your words wide o'er the land
    By telephones, and daily papers,
That always lend a willing hand
    To eulogize your sumptuous capers.

When such harangues gush from your throats,
    We bless your kind fraternal feeling;
We never think you want our votes—
    Oh, no! you'd scorn such double-dealing.
Perhaps a thin-skinned fool like me
    Is envious of my wealthy neighbor;
But come, Messieurs, and soon we'll see
    The blessings found in "honest labor."

I'll be a self-appointed guide,
    And lead you to the various places;
We'll view the looks of high-born pride,
    On all who wear "proud labor's" traces.
'Tis now the welcome hour of noon,
    And here's a shop with groups reclining;
Step in, and we'll discover soon,
    On what these sons of toil are dining.
12

Come, view this dark, inferior bread !
　Be patient, sirs ; what makes you flutter ?
Is it because it weighs like lead ?
　Or just because it lacks of butter ?
All meats are rather scarce, you see ;
　Their butchers must have failed to slaughter.
And here, in lieu of wines or tea,
　They have a pail of "sparkling water."

The meal is o'er ; we'll now prepare
　To hold a little conversation ;
We'll make some spokesman tell the share,
　They get for building up this nation :
" What news, my boys ; How fares the day ?
　Do Plenty's smiles come kindly beaming ?
Does hope shine forth with prosperous ray,
　Around your future pathway gleaming ?

" Ah, yes ! " said one upon whose brow,
　The plow of care cut many a furrow ;
" Bright Hope is smiling on us now,
　And means to do the same to-morrow ;
Our food consists of smiles of Hope ;
　Messieurs, 'tis good, substantial feeding ;
It saves us from the hangman's rope,
　And checks our wounds from constant bleeding.

"What right have we, poor slaves, to frown,
 To dare to think or dare to ponder
On why you cut our wages down,
 Or why our heart-strings burst asunder?
When hunger's pangs our vitals gnaw
 Or when half-clad in freezing weather,
Why shouldn't we bless the glorious law
 That keeps our bodies and souls together?

We're made of Nature's coarsest clay;
 Our wives and brats, why, keep them starving,
Inferior brood—what right have they,
 To grumble while our fates are carving?
Then train your dogs with savage skill,
 To drive the pauper band in fury;
What matter if they one should kill,
 While you can buy the judge and jury?"

The whistle's sound soon ceased the talk;
 With sullen and sarcastic bearing,
Away they went in sullen walk,
 As motionless we stood there, staring.
Messieurs, such movements mean a dire,
 Disastrous, fierce, internal friction,
Which yet may burst in flames of fire,
 Beyond the power of laws' restriction,

COME AND NESTLE UP CLOSELY, MY DARLING.

Come and nestle up closely, my darling!
　　Dearest girl with the long raven hair.
You can sing in my arms like a starling,
　　You delight me when ever you're there.
Let the world wag away with its bother,·
　　While your heart is up closely to mine;
We will whisper fond hopes to each other,
　　For you know I am faithfully thine.

Should the darkness of grief beat around us,
　　And the clouds of misfortune arise, ·
They will ne'er have the power, love, to wound us,
　　They will soon disappear from our skies.
When your lips touch my soul, as I press them,
　　I will drink at the fountain my fill!
With a miserly greed I'll caress them,
　　And I'll keep them as slaves to my will.

When your arms circle round me, my treasure!
　　I will fancy the angels are near;
I'll enjoy ev'ry moment of pleasure,
　　As I list to your pledges sincere.
Then the years may unfold all their sorrows;
　　We have faith to surmount ev'ry ill,
Which shall come with the gloomy to-morrows,
　　For our hearts shall beat truthfully still.

BLIGHTED HOPES.

One night, as in an easy chair
  I sat, perusing mystic lore,
I heard a footstep on the stair,
  Then came a knocking at my door ;
The hour was late, the taper's ray
  Scarce lit the dreary midnight gloom,
Yet, at my call, without delay,
  A visitor stepped in the room.

A man he was, and in his eye
  I marked a sad, peculiar grace,
As if bright hope had passed him by,
  And sought some other resting place ;
His years they numbered manhood's prime ;
  His haggard glance the story told—
That care outstripped the march of Time,
  And made him prematurely old.
I welcomed him and bade him rest,
  He made a common-place reply ;
His voice touched springs within my breast,
  Which long I thought were parched and dry.

" My friend ! and can it really be
  'Tis you, returned home at last,
Who trod life's morning road with me
  In days long numbered with the past ?

Speak out, why leave me in suspense?
    Your voice is all I recognize,
Long days gone by you went from hence,
    And wandered off 'neath stranger skies.''

I paused, and his extended hand
    I clasped with old-time, boyish glee;
I welcomed him to father-land,
    Who, years had roved o'er land and sea.
In failing voice my guest began
    To tell his tale, 'mid falling tears,
How he had strayed, as boy and man,
    Across the waste of many years.
But from his lips the tale must fall;
    Each plaintive note of pent-up grief
My Muse will re-produce, that all
    May read a life-page sad, but brief.

" A score of years have nearly ran
    Their varying, changing course along,
Since I, allured by hope, began
    To mingle with life's struggling throng.
My father's home amongst the trees;
    My mother's reverential air,
As morning, noon, and night, her knees
    Would bend in pious, heart-felt prayer,
For God to bless our humble cot,

And all assembled 'round therein ;
Alas ! too soon they were forgot,
 Exchanged for gilded ways of sin.
Intoxicating draughts I sought,
 I quaffed, too deep, the midnight bowl,
I drained its dregs, but never thought
 How soon I could pollute my soul.
Being cast in Nature's stalwart mould,
 Such word as fear I ne'er have known.
Too fiercely brave, too bravely bold,
 Endowed with muscle, nerve and bone.
I never paused to count the cost
 Of wild debauch on strength and mind ;
Through many golden years I lost,
 I never cast a glance behind.
One day there came in mourning guise
 A little note, 'twas quickly read,
'Mid choking sobs and tear-dimm'd eyes,
 It told my noble sire was dead.
To deeper depths I then went down ;
 I neared the verge of crime's abyss ;
Saw firey eye-balled demons frown ;
 Heard shrieks and groans and serpents hiss.
I fled, the fiends of hell gave chase,
 And on my heels pursued me fast.
 * * * * * * * * *
A mother's prayers soon won the race,
 And reformation came at last !

I started on life's road anew,
   I met a girl of witching grace,
With flowing hair of sunny hue,
   And brilliant mind, and handsome face.
I loved as only man can love,
   I grew a boy at heart again,
And for her sake I fondly wove
   A future bright, untinged by pain.

I crowned her empress of my heart;
   I knelt before her vestal shrine;
And e're we tore ourselves apart,
   She pledged eternal love with mine.
I left her then to seek for fame
   Among the busy haunts of men,
And for her sake to win a name,
   By aid of voice and guileless pen.
She seemed the counterpart of me,
   Her very life, her hopes and fears,
She said within my heart I'd see;
   And note no change in future years.
She then became my guiding star;
   How oft my weary brain has sought
To ward away the conflict's jar,
   By sweet companionship of thought.
My pen was powerless to portray
   Upon the paper's ample page,

My burning love, each closing day;
  The very moments seemed an age,
That I have lingered in suspense,
  Until I'd get a fond reply;
'Twould cheer my heart, and soothe each sense,
  When reading with a gloating eye—
But why prolong this painful theme,
  To scourge my lacerated mind?
'Twas all a curs'd delusive dream,
  That left its venomed stings behind.
E'en now in memory she is near,
  The dirge of by-gone days to toll.
My friend, forgive this falling tear,
  She lured me with a perjured soul.
My peace of mind's forever gone,
  My heart for sweet contentment gropes;
This was the cap-stone placed upon
  My pyramid of blighted hopes."

His words grew incoherent—wild.
  He paused to gain a moment's rest.
Again he raised his head and smiled,
  As hope had dawned within his breast.
"But friend," he said, "our boyhood days
  Have many treasured gems in store,
How oft my retrospective gaze
  Grew bright, amid those scenes of yore.

'Mid joyous scenes of early youth
  My memory often backward stole,
To live again and seek for truth
  In dreamy mansions of the soul.
But past, forever fare-you-well!
  The present has no joy for me,
The future, ah! what tongue can tell
  The joy or grief which in it be?
I recognize the power divine,
  That wraps it up in mystic gloom,
Yet, rays of hope around it shine,
  To light my soul beyond the tomb."

I CANNOT SING TO-NIGHT, LOVE.

I cannot sing to-night, love,
  For I've an aching brow;
I feel affection's blight, love,
  Descending on me now.
I've sipped the nectar sweet, love,
  Upon your lips that grow;
But then, 'twas pleasure fleet, love,
  And now I'm sunk in woe.

I cannot sing to-night, love,
  My voice has lost the charms

Which gave you once delight, love,
  When circled in my arms.
The sweet, delusive thrill, love,
  I felt when you were near
Now feels an aching chill, love,
  From pledges insincere.

I cannot sing to-night, love,
  For all your witching snares,
And features sparkling bright, love,
  Can't win those joyous airs
Which oft I sang to you, love,
  In blissful moments past,
When you have pledged me true, love,
  That joys like those would last.

I cannot sing to-night, love,
  I'm passion-tossed with pain,
I wish you'd leave my sight, love,
  And ease my 'wilder'd brain—
But, stay, your features, dearly,
  Delude me as of yore.
I'll dream you love sincerely,
  And sing you one song more !

OUT OF THE SHOP.

I'm out of the shop, where I've been for repairs;
　　Yes, out of the shop, where I've lingered for
　　　years;
Once more in the cab, putting on all the airs
　　That ever were thought of by gay engineers.
I've got a rebuild of the "monkey-wrench" kind;
　　I've also been "daubed with a bucket of paint;"
And boys, ere the close of this year you shall find
　　I can yet bring a smile to the phiz of a saint.

Where are the old friends whom I've met with
　　of yore?
　　Are all of them yet 'mid earth's turmoil and
　　　strife?
Or have they set brakes on eternity's shore,
　　With trains safely brought up the grades of
　　　this life?
From north, boys, to south, from the west to the
　　east
　　There were many heroes I'll miss from the
　　　throng,
Who've often sat down with myself at a feast,
　　And drained a full glass to my meritless song.

But, boys, I have tears for the graves of our dead;
　　I also have smiles which you plainly can trace,
For each gallant lad who is fighting for bread,

Upon an old mill, with a black smoky face;
Who'll stand in the cab—and with sinews of steel;
If danger's ahead be prepared for the shock—
And then down the bank with his engine he'll reel,
His throttle still clasping, unflinching as rock.

My mother once said: "Arrah, Shandy take care,
And keep out of danger as long as you can;
A hero may die, but, my son, I declare
A coward can live all his days like a man."
I have always been known as a dutiful son;
I'll take her advice when there's danger around;
The heroes may take my whole share of such fun,
For I shall step off on a soft spot of ground.

Keep up your insurance, protect well your lives;
You can't tell the moment old Death with his shears
Shall straggle around and bequeath to your wives
A few thousand dollars to dry up their tears.
Then, boys, how they'll dress in rich billows of black!
With veils drooping down o'er each grief-stricken face;
When once they are sure that you cannot come back
Another will squander the dimes in your place.

Old Time, if I only could hamper your flight,
  Or scatter contentment for all in your wake,
I'd make my old harp-strings melodious to-night,
  And sing a sweet song for the sad hearts that
    ache.
My mission would be 'mid the lowly and poor,
  Whose hunger-pinched faces are haggard and
    thin,
Who scarcely can keep the mad wolf from the
    door,
That comes to devour the half starved ones
    within.

Oh, Lord! it is sad, what we daily behold,
  To see how the poor are derided on earth;
To see how they're tortured with hunger and cold,
  While struggling for life from the moment
    of birth,
With heart-rending pains, and the manifold ills
  That crawl through our frames till we shiver
  . and shake,
With sickness and sorrow, convulsions, and chills,
  Which clasp us as tight as a Westinghouse
    brake.

By gracious! a tear has just rolled from my eyes;
  Old Muse, ere next month you must alter your
    strain,
Soar up, and away, to those bright, sunny skies,

That gleam far above our old 'Castle in Spain.'
'Tis there we can warble in satire and mirth,
And sing undisturbed as we both may desire;
There's not such another dear spot on this earth,
For you, and your frolics, and Shandy Maguire.

BURY THE PAST.

Oh, bury the past, my boys,
Be sure you bury it deep;
If not it will surely rise,
Like ghostly faces in sleep;
I mean the remorseful past,
Which many men call " wild oats,"
If not it will hold you fast,
With vengeful grip at your throats.

When by the style of the years,
Which leads down the vale of life,
Perhaps it may save some tears,
From many a faithful wife;
And don't be at all surprised,
Unless you have hearts of stone,
When keeping the past disguised,
You'll save some tears in your own,

You may count your beads all day,
And mutter your aves out,
To keep the specters away,
If once they're let roam about;
It is best to sink them deep
Where all kindred criminals dwell,
For a long eternal sleep,
If down you should dig to hell.

Then keep from their graves away,
Through all of your future days,
If not, when your head is gray,
A furnace may round you blaze.
This counsel given in rhyme
Should on your memory last,
Perhaps it may guard from crime,
If down you bury the past.

REFLECTIONS ON LIFE.

When the sun of life is shining,
  Ere a cloud begins to rise,
To bedim the glorious lustre
  Of our bright meridian skies,
Then, my boys, we must remember
  That his beams don't always stay,

To enliven up the evening
  Of that fast approaching day,
When the gloomy ills shall gather,
  And with penetrating force,
Travel reckless through our bodies
  In a devastating course;
Bearing daily grim reminders,
  That our manhood's boasted prime,
Is most surely drifting downward
  On the tidal-waves of time.

When the turkey-tracks all gather
  On each florid looking brow,
Where old father Time sits gloating
  'Mid the furrows of his plow;
When the silver threads are streaking
  Through redundant heads of hair, ·
And the rheumatism driving
  Us through torture and despair;
When the belladonna plasters
  Are prescribed to help each back,
As we try to fool the doctor,
  Cursing driving-springs and track;
He will listen quite attentive,
  Should our friends be standing near,
But when once they leave our presence
  He will thunder in each ear:

13

"If you wish to know your ailment,
  I will tell you simple truth,
You are now a holy martyr,
  Caused by piety in youth;
And with bolus, pills, and plasters,
  I shall have to overhaul
The lost motion of your body,
  Or a helpless wreck you'll fall."
What a splendid consolation,
  As we suffer in our grief,
To be told that from our ailments
  There's no permanent relief!

Now, my dinner-pail companions,
  Who mix gold dust in your tea,
Every day, instead of sugar,
  So you'll spend your money free,
Give attention to the future
  As you stroll through summer flowers,
Find a cozy place of shelter,
  From the winter's piercing showers;
Save up all the little trifles,
  Put extravagance to rout,
Keep the crimson from your noses,
  And be careful of the gout.
For with present rates of wages,
  The most skeptic must agree,

If you practice from my precepts
   You'll be millionaires, like me;
And each honest face will brighten
   With a buckled-crown-sheet smile,
As you contemplate your savings,
   When they run you by the mile!
With what thoughts I sit and listen
   To those eloquent divines,
Who drink deep of inspiration
   From the choicest brands of wines!
Which enable them to thunder
   Texts of Scripture in our ears,
Telling how the road to Heaven
   Has been built on human tears;
And the wrecks upon the sidings
   Are a vicious, sinful band
Of garroters and marauders,
   Who'll ne'er see the Promised Land!
Oh! 'tis then I feel rebellion
   Running madly through my veins,
When I think how faint with hunger,
   And 'mid many aches and pains,
How 'mid cold and desolation,
   Or 'mid summer's burning rays,
We must struggle for existence
   Through this world's winding ways;
And when all the fight is over,

As we fall upon the sod—
When the summons is delivered
  To appear before our God—
Then to find the tribulations
  Of the honest, ill-starred poor,
Beside all the dire misfortunes
  We were called on to endure,
Are a mass of bitter curses
  In this life to undergo,
Ere our Maker shall condemn us
  Into everlasting woe;
While our rich and reverend teachers,
  Blest with luxury from birth,
May take sleeping-cars to heaven
  When they're called away from earth !

Ah ! the strife may be unequal
  Here 'mid earthly hills and vales,
But, beyond the tomb, dear reader,
  There's a cherub at the scales,
Who will guard the balance fairly,
  And see justice done to those
Who have fought their way courageous
  'Mid a multitude of foes !

PROSPERITY'S PET.

Miss Fortune, indeed, is a whimsical dame,
  And a difficult damsel for mankind to woo;
She shuffles life's cards, then sits watching the
    game,
  To see the stakes won by her favorite few.
There's one of the winners I've watched for some
    time,
Whose changes we'll trace in the following rhyme.
In girlhood's young years, unassuming and plain,
Till wealth with its joys nearly muddled her brain,
And filled her with moonshiny notions so full,
That good common sense had forsaken her skull.
Put beggars on horseback they'll canter to—well
  You know the old saying, 'tis somewhat pro-
    fane.
Old goosequill, to duty, and truthfully tell
  The reader a tale in satirical strain.

Dear reader 'tis only a few years ago,
  A verdant young girl, named Julia Ann Brown,
Drove a green-grocer cart, up and down, to and
    fro,
  Selling garden produce on the streets of the
    town.
In a calico dress thrifty Judy was clad,
Looking lanky and lean, without bustle or pad,
To the apings of fashion and dressmaker's art

She was wholly unknown, perched aloft on her
    cart,
Selling onions, tomatoes, beans, turnips, and
    squash,
Adding dimes into dollars and hoarding the cash.
The years sped along o'er this vender of greens,
And Judy sped with them away from her teens.
Prosperity smiled.   The potato-bug swarm
Dealt havoc around, but avoided her farm;
The harvest arrived, and a plentiful store
Of potatoes gave Judy the ducats galore.

Since then there's a change in the life of Miss
    Brown.
The upstart aspires to be belle of the town.
I saw her last Sunday, she stood in the porch,
Arranging her dress to parade into church;
Then onward she went with a butter-milk smile,
And a strut like a goose, up the carpeted aisle.
She was late by design, so her style we could
    view,
And the length of her train as she went to her
    pew.
Bending o'er in devotion devoutly she sat,
    While all in that vast congregation did stare
At the beautiful plume that she wore in her hat,
    As she seemed to be wholly absorbed in her
        prayer.

Ah, Judy! I wish I could teach you a truth,
  That art with its minions may labor in vain
To give to your features the freshness of youth,
  Or temper the public's cold glance of disdain,
Too long have you peddled your wares on the
    street,
And bantered away with each housewife you'd
    meet,
To think we'd forget what you were when you
    rode .
  In your father's old coat, buttoned up to keep
    warm,
Each cold chilly day on the top of a load
  Of potatoes and pumpkins you raised on the
    farm.

TIME'S VISIT.

One night I sat in dreamy mood,
  Enwrapped in semi-gloom,
No living soul did there intrude
  Within my cozy room.
The embers in the little grate
  Were dying, one by one,
As there I sat, to meditate
  On days long passed and gone.

Each fading spark my fancy wove,
   Until it did appear
Like some old friend, I once did love,
   With friendship most sincere;
In happy days, long passed and gone,
   Which I shall always prize,
Before the clouds of care rolled on
   To dim those morning skies.

I dreamed in semi-concious state,
   'Till drowsiness did creep;
And, as the last spark left the grate,
   My eyes were closed in sleep;
How long I slept I cannot tell,
   Perhaps an hour or more,
'Till roused up by the midnight bell
   And knocking at the door.

Perhaps some poor, belated man,
   Is seeking fire and food;
To let him in, I quickly ran,
   He'd share my solitude;
The bolt flew back, there stepped within
   That little, cozy place,
A curious being, with a grin
   Upon his wrinkled face!

In speechless awe I mutely gazed,
    Until the stranger spoke ;
" Rouse up ! don't seem so much amazed,
    I came to have a smoke,
And chat awhile with you, my lad ;
    For we've been friends for years ;
You've known me when your heart was glad
    And also in your tears."

" My name is Time, you know me now ?"
    " Ah, yes," I said in fright,
" Your mark is here upon my brow,
    I thought of you to-night ;
In fact, you're ever in my mind."
    He then replied : " Much crime
In all your dreamy moods I find,
    Wherein you slaughter Time."

" You drive along in reckless haste,
    You never stop to pause
Upon the many hours you waste,
    You disregard my laws ;
But, know you, I will win the race,
    Although your strides are fleet ;
Effectively I will efface
    The earth-marks of your feet.

Like many more, you think you've got
  A lease of endless joy ;
I called such foolish thoughts to blot
  From out your brain, my boy.
You'll find the years will roll along
  With steady, noiseless tread,
And lay their cygnet mark upon
  Your visionary head.

I've traveled from creation's birth,
  Adown the countless years,
Which swiftly flew across the earth ;
  I've witnessed human tears,
Enough to make an ocean, vast
  As space between the polls ;
And noticed untold wrecks drift past
  Of lost, despairing souls.

"For youth my measured pace is slow,
  Their blood in surging tides
Keep bounding, with resistless flow,
  To urge their headlong strides.
Age supplicates me to delay ; ,
  My speed exhausts his breath,
And when he falls 'longside the way,
  He's gathered in by Death."

"Yourself is not so anxious now
  To see the seasons fly
As when bright curls o'er your brow
  Half hid each dancing eye.
You've sobered down, and love the fire,
  Besides, an easy chair,
And peevishly, in churlish ire,
  You wrangle much with Care."

"Behold that puff of smoke ascend,
  And now it disappears;
'Tis fleet as human life, my friend,
  And prototypes the years;
They come, they go, and puny man,
  With all his boasted skill,
Has but a lease of briefest span,
  His mission here to fill.

"Don't think—like other hair-brained fools,
  In every age and clime—
You can defy my golden rules,
  And steal a march on Time.
I'll be a victor o'er the graves
  Of all the human race,
And I'll conceal, 'neath murky waves,
  Their earthly resting place."

He ceased, and vanished from my sight,
　　Just as the streaks of day
Were penetrating through the night,
　　With tints of morning's gray.
In sadness I reflected on
　　The many things he said,
Before I threw myself upon
　　My uninviting bed.

───

A VISION OF THE NIGHT.

T'other night I had a vision,
　　And it filled me with surprise.
Sure I dreamt I was transported
　　Far away beyond the skies,
Till, just outside Heaven's portals,
　　I was placed with tender care,
And I knocked and sought admission
　　Into blissful mansions there.

Soon the gates were slowly opened
　　By a sanctimonious chap,
Who demanded what I wanted
　　In my greasy clothes and cap.

I explained and gently told him
    That I "read my title clear"
Down on earth among the snow-drifts,
    As a half starved engineer.

"Come right in, my worthy brother,"
    Said St. Peter, "I am sure
That I've never punched a ticket
    Since I've stood upon this door,
Half so worthy of admission
    As this one you bring to hand,
From the snow-drifts and poor steamers
    Of that northern Yankee land."

I was dazzled with the splendor
    I beheld on every side !
I was placed within a chariot,
    And was given quite a ride
'Round among some lucky angels,
    Who for twenty years in mirth,
Have been residents of Heaven,
    Since I missed them from the earth.

Oh ! I recognized old timers,
    Who blasphemed in days gone by,
When they were detained for orders,
    Or on sidings had to lie ;

And I asked the saintly Peter
    How they got in Paradise.
He replied: "By running scrap-piles
    With the flanges full of ice."

"Are there any kid-gloved-gentry
    Here on Canaan's happy shore;
Such as ten-per-cent-reducers,
    Of the panic days of yore?"
Then his scowl looked liked the Heavens
    When tornados fiercely blow,
As he shook his saintly noddle,
    And just pointed down below!

"Are there any applications
    For admission through your gates,
From among some gay conductors,
    Who have charge of local freights?"
Said the Saint: "They come here begging,
    But I take a loaded club
And I knock them down to blazes,
    Where they're caught by Beelzebub."

Sure he made me so delighted,
    That I asked him in a joke,
If he'd switch aside the chariot,
    Till we'd have a social smoke.

Oh ! he answered me quite gayly,
　And his smile was most serene :
" Yes, I'd thank you kindly Shandy,
　For a whiff from your dudeen."

There we sat and smoked together,
　Like a jolly pair of boys.
" 'Tis the first time," said his Saintship,
　" That I've tasted Heaven's joys ;
Your old pipe is so delicious
　That it kind o' roils my head."
" Smoke it slowly, then, my bouchal,
　And may Heaven be your bed.

" Are there many dead-head tickets
　Here presented at the gate ? "
" Yes, my boy ; I've counted millions,
　But l quickly seal their fate ;
They come up and try to pass me,
　Just because their dying day
Is employed donating treasure
　Which they cannot bring away."

" Are there any railroad supers
　'Round about us to be seen ? "
" They are like hen's teeth," said Peter,
　" Very few, and far between,"

" Where are all those train despatchers
  Who could pull so many cars ? "
" They are down below my hearty,
  With their noses through the bars."

" Can you tell me if you ever
  Saw the patentee come in,
Of the famous Mack injector ? "
  Sure the Saint began to grin.
" Yes, my boy ; he's quite convenient
  To the place we're sitting here.
And his pass read : ' Benefactor
  To the railroad engineer ! ' "

" Do you ever have directors
  From a road that pays in scrip ? "
" No, indeed, I don't," said Peter,
  " They all take a downward trip ! "
" Well, from roads of heavy traffic,
  Where they pay us by the mile ? "
" Do you take me for a booby ? "
  Said his Saintship, with a smile.

" Oh, be gor ! I don't, your honor,
  Though I never went to school,
I can tell by looking at you
  That you're far from being a fool ;

Yet, I thought I'd ask a question,
   As I know of two now dead,
Whom I swear could beat the devil."
" They're still with him ! " Peter said.

" I suppose you're bother'd hourly,
   By poor suffering millionaires,
Who must do some honest labor ·
   Climbing up the golden stairs ? "
" No, I never have a caller,
   For old Charon with his tricks,
Locks them up in summer villas,
   Right across the river Styx."

" Are there any politicians
   Scattered here among the stars ? "
" Nary one ! " said honest Peter,
   " We could never stand their jars."
" I suppose you're full of preachers,
   Who have taught us how to pray ? "
" You're mistaken," he responded,
   " There are thousands drove away."

" There's a spring of living waters,
   At whose Christianizing fount
Flows a gospel universal,
   Named ; 'The Sermon on the Mount.'
      14

Those not preaching it find regions
    Where there's not a flake of snow;
And I pledge my saintly honor,
    There the hypocrites must go."

When the smoking made him drowsy
    I commit a fatal sin;
Heaven's keys I pilfered from him,
    Till I'd let poor spirits in.
At my slightest touch the wickets
    Widely opened in the sky.
Holy Moses! what a racket!
    As the ladies passed me by.

Soon ten thousand peals of thunder
    O'er the heavens fiercely roared!
And St. Peter ran terrific,
    Armed with a flaming sword;
He drove back the fair invaders,
    And I crouched in mortal fear,
As the weapon gleamed above me,
    While he shouted in my ear:

"Oh, you unrepentent rascal!
    Since the earth was launched in space,
'Tis the first time woman's prattle
    E'er assailed this sacred place?"

Then the flaming sword descended ;
　As I jumped to dodge the stroke,
In a lethargy bewildered,
　From the vision I awoke.

CHURCH ‑MUSINGS.

Thank God, the forty days of Lent,
That He to punish us has sent,
　　Are quickly rolling on,
And ere these lines are told to drink
Their modest draught of printer's ink,
　　Once more shall Lent be gone.

For many weeks, with hungry moans,
I've masticated myriad bones
　　Of every kind of fish;
I've cut, and slashed, and hacked and chewed
Through all the schools of scaly food
　　That penitent could wish.

The bones are piercing through my skin,
Alas! I feel a dorsal fin
　　Protruding 'neath my vest!
Their gills, and scales, and slimy eyes,
Like ghosts around my bed arise,
　　To break my needed rest.

My throttle arm's growing weak,
The lever I can scarcely take
    A hold of like a man.
The track is rough, I roll around,
Until I swear at every bound,
    As lusty as I can.

A solid dish of pork and beans,
Or bacon, fried in juicy greens,
    Would make my eye-balls roll;
I think 'twould drive away more sin,
Than all I prayed since Lent came in;
    I do, upon my soul!

Oh! for a steak cut from a hog,
Or off a cow, or yonder dog,
    Ah, yes, or from a cat,
A horse, a mule, a goat, an ass—
I swear, this moment by the mass
    I'd masticate a rat!

The church forbids, and I must starve,
A piece of meat I dare not carve,
    Or I incur her bans;
Gaunt hunger has a deadly gripe
Unless on suction, like a snipe,
    I feed, and foil her plans.

The Bible says to fast and pray,
'Twas thus my pastor preached one day.
    My pastor tells no fibs.
Poor man! he looks as though he takes
His penance out in sirloin steaks,
    While I pick codfish ribs.

I know the good man loves me well,
Far better than my pen can tell,
    For he has told me so.
He said to fast; if not, my crimes,
Together with my railing rhymes,
    Would land me down below.

Since then at church I'm always found,
I very seldom glance around,
    Except some saint comes in,
Whose features wear a dainty smile,
Parading up the middle aisle,
    To purge herself from sin.

Those saints I find wear seal-skin sacques,
With ermine trimm'd well down their backs,
    And hats of gorgeous plumes;
I likewise note they're always late,
And strut along with peacock gait
    To pews where fashion blooms.

I wonder if they feed on fish,
Or on a more ethereal dish
    Of sighs and saintly groans?
Perhaps to buy their gaudy silk
They starve themselves on mush and milk
    Or caudled codfish bones.

My creed requires much penitence,
For every simple, slight offense
    Committed in the flesh;
Dear knows, the man who pulls a train
In heat and cold, in shine and rain,
    May scorn the church's lash.

I like a sermon short and sweet,
But not a theologic treat,
    Beyond my simple reach;
I also love the fervent zeal
An honest man is sure to feel
    Who'll practice what he'll preach.

I like to sit and criticise
The man who'll preach translators' lies,
    With sactimonious ire;
Who tells us that beyond the grave
Our sinful souls must always lave
    In seas of liquid fire.

When Gabriel's trump shall wake the dead,
I know that those who toiled for bread
    Need have no cause to fear;
I truly think our Lord on high
Will give us rest beyond the sky
    For what we suffered here.

THE HOMEWARD BOUND.

The seaman's song is blithe and free,
He leaves the "Goodwins" on his lee.
His ship is trim, her sails expand
With gentle breezes from the land.
All hands on deck the yards do square,
To waft her through the waves and air.
Now, all is clear, the harbor passed,
And bending o'er each lofty mast;
The studding-sails are quickly spread,
And in the chains one heaves the lead,
    The channel's depths to sound;
The pilot hears his answers shrill,
Which forth he sends with right good will.
The chorus of his shipmates tell
That all on board are going well,
    And they are homeward bound.

For two long years on ocean wide
They've battled with the winds and tide.
They've sailed along its liquid blue,
From frozen Greenland to Peru.
Been buffeted in Arctic seas,
And bronzed by many a tropic breeze.
Exposed to gales and hot simoons,
And wafted onward by monsoons.
In Bay of Biscay lost a spar,
Besides their most courageous tar.
Fought pirates on the Spanish Main,
Till all were captured, drowned, or slain.
The stars and stripes at mast-head high
Oft floated 'neath a foreign sky;
And weary pilgrims paused to see
Their country's flag still flying free;
Her ships well manned, both staunch and true,
And fit to cleave the waters blue.
From out a distant port her bow
Is pointed to the west-ward now,
      And songs aloft resound.

The pilot takes his leave when she
Is many leagues upon the sea.
Her course is set, the watch remains
On deck to view the steady strains
Upon each yard, each boom, each rope.

Their hearts exult with joyous hope,
    For they are homeward bound.

A little while and they'll behold
Their native land its shores unfold,
To bless the sight of those who viewed
Old ocean's face in solitude ;
Or seen the mighty billows rise
In madd'ning leap at angry skies ;
Like liquid Alps, their crests of spray
Picked up and swirl'd in flakes away.
A little while and kindred dear
Will greet them with a love sincere.
The Yankee girls will take in tow
Their noble ship with glad heave, ho !
The steersman as he leaves the wheel,
Responds in words his messmates feel,
    When his relief comes round :
"Her course is west, Jack, keep her full,
Make every stitch of canvas pull.
Ball off the knots with willing hand,
Until the look-out spies the land,
    For we are homeward bound."

And now the water's em'rald sheen
Is changing to a darker green.
The land birds perch upon the stays ;

And drift-wood floats from out the bays.
The coasters cross their wake and tell
That all on board are doing well.
The decks are holy-stoned with care;
And men are swung in upper air,
To make all ready for the coast,
Where seamen fear the danger most.
Suspense upon their features creep,
And very few on board can sleep—
For know you, landsmen, nearing home,
When over leagues of sea you roam,
There is a fear which steals within
The lightest heart, that loves its kin—
That some dear form you may not spy,
From whom you went with tear-dimm'd eye;
Some hearth may have a vacant chair,
Since off you sailed from loved ones there;
      Perhaps beneath a mound,
Your father or your mother true
May sleep, whose parting breath, for you
Was sent to God to guard you well,
With love far more than tongue can tell,
      And wished you homeward bound.

But see! The ensign's at the peak,
A passing ship they're going to speak.
Ha! ha! Their longitude is right,

And soon they'll have the beach in sight.
The frenzied glances of the crew
Can't penetrate the hazy hue
Which settles on the ocean's breast,
Until the sun glides down the west,
And sends bright beams athwart the sky
Through vapors dense that on it lie.
Eight bells are tolled.   The watch is called.
The ground-gear now is overhauled;
The anchors catted on the rail,—
But, hark! what means that joyous hail?
"Land ho!" the look-out wildly cries,
"Land ho!" the second mate replies.
The captain with his glass now goes
Aloft to see its shape disclose,
He sings his orders quick and clear,
And tells the wheelsman how to steer,
For Sandy Hook is drawing near,
And soon they'll be with kindred dear,
        On well remember'd ground.
They drive away all frenzied fear,
Care from their bosoms disappear;
They dash him on his ghostly bier,
Without a pang, without a tear;
Suspense gives way to joy sincere,
        For they are homeward bound.

Familiar objects on the shore
Are pointed out, by those once more,
Who viewed them weary months before,
When seaward their staunch frigate bore;
Whose keel plowed nobly on her course,
And triumphed o'er the billow's force;
Until she now rides safe and sound,
With anchors down in holding ground.
At last the voyage is complete,
And *terra firma* 'neath their feet.
The salutation : "All is well,"
The fears of those on board dispel.
    Each loving friend is found.
In fond embrace they're warmly clasped,
And many hands are stoutly grasped,
    To greet the homeward bound.

TO CALDWELL B. BENSON, ON HIS TRAVELS.

You're now upon a foreign shore,
In lands beyond Atlantic's roar,
    'Mid objects European.
Perhaps, as here I sit and sing,
You're hob-a-nobbing with a king,
    Or waltzing with his queen.

Where'er you are I'll safely bet,
Columbia's shore you'll ne'er forget—
  The land which gave you birth.
You'll find she stands the first of all
The nations, whether great or small,
  To-day upon the earth.

You are a man whose liberal mind
Is honest, broad, and not confined
  Within contracted bounds;
You'll note, when moving on your tour,
The gulf dividing rich and poor,
  On Europe's slavish grounds.

You'll find those titled things they call
Lords, dukes and earls, creatures all
  Of very common clay;
Who think they have a perfect right
To trample o'er, by force of might,
  God's poor who block their way.

Perhaps upon yourself they'll sneer,
Or on your native land, so dear
  To every honest heart;
If so, they'll find your free-born soul
Will fly beyond your calm control,
  Revengeful, ere you part,

Where'er in courts of wealth or fame
You'll chance to meet a titled dame,
    Compare her with your wife;
More graceful lines you'll plainly trace
Upon her noble, handsome face,
    Than elsewhere during life.

Her features are the truest chart
That ever yet indexed a heart,
    Where Virtue's treasures reign;
Her social smile, her stately mien,
Will envied be by many a queen,
    O'er Europe's broad domain.

I haven't either time or space
Within this book, or I would trace
    Some sights along your route;
Of cities numbered with the dead;
Of fields where ghostly warriors tread,
    Which I have read about.

Tread lightly on green Erin's sod,
'Tis nurtured with the martyr's blood,
    Through centuries of wrong;
On every hill, on every plain,
On rivers rolling to the main,
    Her life's tide flows along.

Her sons aspire to make her free,
They will not bend a slavish knee,
 In this enlightened age.
They've struggled long with little hope;
The headman's axe, the hangman's rope,
 Disgrace her history's page.

On England's old, historic soil,
You'll find reward for all your toil,
 Amid her wealth and fame.
You'll see the splendor, pomp and glare,
Of all that mighty nation there,
 Around her laureled name.

When Scotland's skies are o'er your head,
Oh, think upon the mighty dead
 Who sleep within her womb!
Move gently o'er the sacred ground
Where pilgrims walk in reverence round
 Famed Bobbie Burns' tomb.

Your piercing, keen, observing glance,
Shall note luxurious sights in France,
 And flash with joy in Spain.
Italian sights are truly grand,
Where art and nature, hand in hand,
 Parade in gorgeous train.

In German States find out the cause
Why they enact such stringent laws
    Against our Yankee pork;
Our juicy hams, well fried in eggs,
Would cure old Bismarck's gouty legs,
    If cooked a la New York.

In Russia keep a sharp look out
For victims of a tyrant's knout;
    If not you'll feel a jar.
Such princely looking men as you,
Beneath her flag are very few;
    They'll take you for the Czar.

Too long I've spun this tedious rhyme,
Or I would rove through every clime
    'Neath Europe's azure dome
With you, who know if ladies' smiles
Possess one-half the witching wiles
    Of melting maids at home.

I love you, " Cad," your heart is warm;
E'en foes admire your manly form
    And independent mind;
Oh, how I love the sterling ring
Your voice contains, as forth you spring,
    On cliques of every kind!

Your wealth is not the miser's hoard,
You never keep your riches stored,
    Secure with locks and keys;
You'll fling it from your open hand,
Amongst the poor in every land
    Beyond our Yankee seas.

We sadly miss your genial face
From every dear, accustomed place
    It used to be of yore;
And may the months speed quickly by,
Until your welcome form we'll spy
    Upon our trains once more.

When westward bound, with favoring gales,
Some swift Cunarder spreads her sails
    To bring your party back;
I hope she'll cleave her liquid way,
Triumphant o'er old ocean's spray,
    Upon the starboard tack.

And when the gang-plank's shoved ashore,
To land you 'mongst your friends once more
    Upon Manhattan's strand;
I hope you'll find the brightest gem
Of all the nation's diadem
    Your own dear native land.

15

ADMIRATION.

"What is there to admire in me?"
   A Juno said in tones serenely,
"Come tell me everything you see."
   She uttered with a precept queenly.

"I see the counterpart of one
I think as bright as mid-day sun;
Whose cheeks are blooming as the rose,
Which in some tropic garden grows;
Whose eyes are brighter than the stars
Called Venus, Mercury, or Mars;
Whose breath is sweet as morning dew,
Or spicy zephyrs of Peru;
Whose hands are slender, small, and soft,
Who smiles like angels up aloft;
Who glides as graceful as the swan,
   Her every attitude and motion
In you combine, then handsome one,
   That's why I tender my devotion.

If I were only fancy free,
   And met you on life's early morning,
My loving heart would sing in glee,
   And win you 'spite of all your scorning;
I'd tune my harp to simple lays,
Both night and day I'd sing your praise,

I'd not be conquered by despair,
Faint heart ne'er won a lady fair.
I'd never hesitate or falter,
Until I had you at the altar;
And then adown the tide of life,
  Its hand in hand we'd go together,
When sailing off the rocks of strife,
  We'd float as buoyant as a feather.

My worthy friend, why do you ask?
  Why put me to this pleasant task?
Yet, if I had time and leisure,
I'd answer more with greatest pleasure;
I'd tell you every reason why
You're fairest 'neath this August sky.
Your mirror will reflect to you
  When next before its face you stand
A queenly shape, to Nature true
  As any from her skillful hand.

RETROSPECTION.

How I love to sit and ponder
  On the happy days of yore,
When the wine of life raced freely
  From an unexhausted store;

When we battered Care's old castle
  With a hearty fusilade
Of sweet songs and merry laughter,
  'Till a breach was in it made.

How the mind must be surrounded
  With a guilty coat of mail,
That will not look back with pleasure
  To some youthful sunlit vale;
Where was raised the joyous chorus
  Of bare-footed boys at play,
As we danced amid the heather
  On a sunny summer's day.

Through the misty clouds of vision
  Hovering o'er maturer years,
I can see the winding river,
  Till my eyes o'erflow with tears;
I can view those happy frolics,
  And the mountain clad in green,
And the sweep of blooming heather
  Where the lambkins played between.

O'er the river's crystal waters
  Like a sea-fowl we could swim;
We disdained the timid cowards
  Who sat shiv'ring on its brim;

O'er the mountain lay the world—
  The horizon of our hopes—
And we burned with rash impatience
  Till we'd pass its grassy slopes.

We have passed them, drifting onward,
  Drifting downward with the years !
Drifting o'er life's troubled ocean,
  With our freight of hopes and fears !
Sometimes tossed on mountain billows,
  Sometimes on calm waters bore,
Yet, we're drifting—ever onward—
  To the undiscovered shore !

There are islands in the ocean,
  Where we sometimes step on land,
To enjoy a few brief moments,
  With a transient, stranger band.
But, alas ! the hours of pleasure
  Which we spare to sport as men,
Make our bark but sail the faster
  When we step on board again.

All the hopes of youth have vanished,
  All its innocence has fled ;
In the struggle for existence,
  We have selfishness instead.

In the tussle and the jostle
    To secure some petty prize,
We tramp down our weaker playmates
    Every morning we arise.

All the treasure of this world—
    And I write the honest truth—
I would give, were I the owner,
    To renew my vanished youth;
To recall those dear companions,
    Who have wandered to and fro,
From the play-ground, near the mountain,
    Since the halcyon long ago!

———

THE BATTLE OF THE CLANS.

RESPECTFULLY INSCRIBED TO THE MAYOR AND MEMBERS OF THE
COMMON COUNCIL.

At sunrise every morning here,
From March 'till cold and bleak December,
    A sound familiar strikes the ear,
Once heard you'll ever more remember.
    It comes from flocks of pigs and geese,
That have this corporation's freedom,
    To roam at large where e'er they please,
Or where their chief marauders lead 'em.

On choicest spots of tender green,
Where care bestowed her longest hours,
　Those daring outlaws may be seen,
When gorging on rare plants and flowers.
　And when their appetites are staid,
The day's diversion soon will follow;
　In battle-lines quite soon arrayed,
Extending over hill and hollow.

　The pigs act umpires of the fight,
Or guard their rear from dogs and cattle
　That interfere, by powerful might,
To end a long and tedious battle.
　This morning perched upon a tree
I took a careful observation,
　For you, Messieurs, who guard this free,
Indulgent, patient, corporation.

　Each flock is known by stride and squeal;
Here comes a clan called "Gosling Alleys."
　The fight begins, around they wheel
To meet voracious Platner valleys.
　With fierce attack they charge the foe,
On flying feet and wings extended;
　At double-quick they onward go,
'Till all are in one dust-cloud blended!

Now comes a lean and lanky clan
To re-inforce the Gosling Alleys;
  It looks as if a goose-Sedan
Awaited all the Platner valleys.
  They enfilade from Duck Egg lane;
A brood of pigs behind them follow.
  Their ganders play a martial strain,
And lead the way to Corky-Hollow.

  Again the contest is renewed.
With beaks and wings, both fast and furious,
  The Gosling Alleys, unsubdued,
Extend their lines with tactics curious.
  But hark! What means that lusty shout?
Up Hoody-Town a band discourses;
  It is the Green Road legion out,
To join the Platner valley forces!

  They wheel in line and open fire;
The Racker-Roads prepare to meet 'em;
  The Hoody-Hills, with keen desire,
And clad in Duck-Creek armor, greet 'em;
  The Green Road geese on flanks and rear,
Attack the half-starved Gosling Alleys—
  The field is won! that lusty cheer
Comes from victorious Platner valleys!

'Tis thus they fight from day to day;
When shades of night around them gather,
  On streets and walks they'll march away,
Without the loss of beak or feather.
  They'll forage on the choicest green
We have in garden or on border;
  A foul and filthy brood, unclean,
Whose owners laugh at law and order.

UNION MEETING AT ROCHESTER, N. Y.

By the clear and placid waters
  Of Ontario at rest,
Where the snowy wings of commerce
  Gently glide upon its breast,
I am sitting, meditating,
  Looking skyward to the moon,
With the memories around me
  Of the fifth and sixth of June.

Oh, ye gods! who favor mortals
  In each laudable desire,
Aid my efforts, I implore you,
  Send one flash of Nature's fire

To illuminate the chambers
 Of my dull, insipid brain,
Till I sing to distant Brothers,
 In an easy, truthful strain.

It was June, and 'mid its roses,
 We enjoyed two days in mirth,
Our surroundings bloomed and blossomed ;
 'Twas a paradise on earth.
Nature donned her grandest raiment;
 In resplendent robes of green ¦
She received our brawny heroes,
 And entranced them with the scene.

Syracuse clasped hands with Brothers
 Up at Rochester, and space
Never yet contained a party
 Who displayed such royal grace ;
'Twas a regal entertainment,
 Gotten up with greatest care,
So 'twould leave a life's impression
 On the guests assembled there.

And the frosts of many seasons
 Were dispelled amid the glow
Of fraternal smiles of welcome,
 From the friends of long ago ;

There were hand-clasps and heart-greetings,
  Such as only men display,
Who exchange the post of duty
  For the pleasures of a day.

Poets sing of orange bowers,
  And of tropic songsters, too,
And of spicy zephyrs blowing
  In the valleys of Peru ;
But they never saw the glories
  Of our northern summer clime,
When the Brotherhood assembles
  For a pleasurable time.

Heaven carpeted our ball-room
  With a spread of velvet green,
And the beaming smiles of beauty
  Gave enchantment to the scene.
There we went through mazy dances
  Till the glorious god of day
Rose with golden smiles to greet us,
  Ere we thought of going away.

And our banquet hall outrivaled
  Fable scenes in fairy land,
Where enchantment loads the tables
  By a magical command.

It surpassed all former efforts
  Of the Brotherhood at large ;
I appeal to Grand Chief Arthur,
  To sustain me in the charge.

'Tis a green spot in the desert
  Of our ever active lives
When we meet for recreation
  With our children and our wives ;
When we lay aside the troubles
  Which beset our paths as men,
And 'mid innocent amusements,
  We can feel as boys again.

———

SIT YOU DOWN AT MY SIDE.

Sit you down at my side
  Till I whisper awhile ;
Let your heart open wide,
  On your face put a smile ;
For I see you are sad,
  There's a cloud on your brow,
And your features are clad
  In dejection just now.

All the moments you spend
　　In gloom, nursing your pain,
Hurries onward your end,
　　They press down on the brain;
All the smiles you put on,
　　Drive the wrinkles away—
Let me see you wear one,
　　Change the night into day.

Sure this life, love, is brief,
　　And your charms soon will fade;
Do not linger in grief,
　　Like a surly old maid;
But attend to the words
　　Which I'll quickly impart,
Like the warbling of birds,
　　Let them steal to your heart.

There's a time to be sad,
　　'Tis when I am not near,
There's a time to be glad,
　　When I'm with you, my dear;
There's a time when you'll sigh,
　　'Tis when wishing for me;
When I come let each eye
　　Speak in welcoming glee.

Ah ! my love, now your face
　　Is with pleasure aglow;
On your brow I can trace
　　Where the love blossoms blow;
And your lips wear a tint
　　Of carnation so bright,
Where my kisses I'll print
　　In profusion to-night.

IN MEMORIAM.

James A. McCarthy, Killed on his Engine at Carlyon,
July 27th, 1883.

'Mid the terrible booming of thunder,
　　Sharp lightning and deluge of rain,
Came the tidings of death and disaster
　　To Carlyon's ill-fated train;
Where the wind's sudden rise in its fury,
　　Soon blew in a merciless gale,
And sent flying along from the siding
　　A car to spread death on the rail.

'Twas a night when the bravest might falter
　　With heartstricken fear and despair,
For it seemed as if legions of demons,
　　Were out and at war in the air;

But the tide of humanity flowing,
　　O'ercame every feeling of fright,
In the rescuing party who labored
　　So bravely that terrible night.

'Twas a sight that shall ne'er be forgotten,
　　While reason presides in the brain,
To behold all the dead and the dying,
　　Who rode on that ill-fated train ;
Heaven pity them all ! Here's one other,
　　Whose equals on earth were but few ;
He's my noble professional brother,
　　Who proved what a brave man can do.

All the newspapers called him a hero,
　　Who bravely met death at his post ;
Ah, yes ! he remained on his engine,
　　To liter'ly broil and to roast.
Not a selfish thought entered his bosom,
　　He stood on the foot-board resigned,
With the lever reversed in the quadrant,
　　To save the three hundred behind.

His poor fireman was pulled out dismembered
　　From under the wreck where it lay,
And he, too, played the part of a hero ;
　　In fragments they bore him away.

They were there like true comrades together,
  Their lifetides besprinkled the sod,
And within a few hours of each other,
  Both spirits ascended to God.

Hurry, Fame, with your brightest of laurels,
  To deck poor McCarthy's last bed ;
He is gone beyond earthly assistance,
  And lies with the heroic dead ;
He is one of the army of victims
  Whom duty requires every year
To be foremost where danger lies thickest,
  And die like a brave engineer.

Hear the multitudes wail as we bear him
  All covered with flowers to the grave ;
Note the grief of his kindred who'd tear him
  Away from the ranks of the brave ;
See his five little, fatherless children,
  Who huddle up close at the bier ;
Hear the sobs of his heart-broken widow,
  Who weeps for the dead engineer.

He is now laid at rest, and forever,
  He sleeps his last sleep 'neath the sod ;
All the wails of his loved ones shall never
  Recall his free spirit from God.

When on duty he never did falter—
  Although he loved children and wife—
But laid down his all on its altar,
  And, mind you, that all was his life.

Oh! I know glorious deeds are recorded
  Above with a merciful pen ;
And I know that all those are rewarded
  Who act as the savers of men.
When the archangel's trumpet gives warning,
  To call up the heroic dead
For review on eternity's morning,
  Brave "Jimmie" will march at the head.

POUR OUT A GOODLY CUP OF CHEER.

Pour out a goodly cup of cheer,
  And quaff its contents down ;
Now out upon the sea we'll steer,
  Although the skies may frown.
My bark is staunch, her hull and sails
  Were built for stormy tides ;
Perhaps she'll meet destructive gales,
  Ere back to port she rides.

Ha ! ha ! the land is fading fast,
　The cloud-rack sweeps the sky ;
The harbor lights are quickly past,
　The seas run mountains high.
My crew are of that mettle made,
　Who stand with bated breath ;
All gallant tars, and not afraid
　To face the monster—death.

The thunder peal vibrates o'erhead,
　The lightning flashes free ;
No soundings with the deep-sea-lead
　On weather or on lee.
The piping winds, like giants hoarse,
　Amid the cordage roar !
But still we steer our seaward course,
　Full many leagues from shore.

This driving pace begins to tell.
　The goodly timbers creak,
Across the decks roll ev'ry swell,
　And soon she'll spring a leak,
Unless the larboard watch is called
　On deck to shorten sail ;
Brave hearts ! they're up and unappalled,
　To fight the roaring gale !

The royals now are safely stowed,
   And our to'gallants too ;
But, see ! from off the yard is blowed
   The bravest of my crew ;
No human aid can save his life,
   He sinks beneath the wave,
Where, undisturbed by mortal strife,
   He'll fill a sailor's grave.

  *   *   *   *   *   *   *   *   *

The clouds begin to drift away,
   And on our weather-beam,
The sun sends down a cheering ray,
   Which on the waters gleam ;
It tells us that all dangers o'er ;
   And calmly we may glide
Across the placid seas once more,
   Upon old ocean wide.

EVENING CHIMES.

When the smoke wreaths ascend in a cloud
   round my nose,
Is the time I enjoy a delicious repose ;
And I bask in the smiles which my fancy creates,
On this cool, balmy eve, when the wide open gates

Of my fancy are flung, to permit me to stray
Where I choose, till the wreaths have all faded
    away;
And the whiffs, like the puffs of a clean-cut
    exhaust,
Circle 'round in the air till in distance they're lost.

I've been reading the *Journal* and found as I read
Intellectual treats from contributors spread
O'er its pages, where Mind is the monarch that
    reigns
In its columns, endowed with his quota of brains.
When we're roasting with heat or when freezing
    with cold,
It brings joy to our hearts every line we behold,
From those kind and affectionate ladies, whose
    lives
Are united with ours, and signed "engineer's
    wives."

When we leave them and bid them a tender good-
    bye,
How the tears trickle down from each "plug-
    puller's" eye,
As we give them a sad and disconsolate kiss,
Knowing well how the poor darling creatures
    we'll miss
When we're off at the other far end of our route,

Where we never were known to go strolling
    about,
But remain in our cabs making pious complaints
To our Maker and reading the Lives of the Saints.

Should we ever come back with a red hair or two
On the sleeves of our coats and exposed to the
    view
Of our wives, who have long raven tresses, why,
    then,
Heaven pity us all, we're unfortunate men!
Don't they know in their hearts how the smoke
    and the gas
Of our engines can color the paint-work and
    brass?
And, of course, 'tis the very same process which
    led
To the change in their own hair they fancied was
    red.

I have never yet heard of the slightest reliance
A woman would place on the wonders of science.
She can talk with a truly intelligent mind
O'er a wide range of topics, with learning refined,
But when once her keen eyes get the sight of a
    hair,
Which she thinks, in her foolishness, shouldn't be
    there;
Oh! it don't matter much if the color be gray,

All her learning takes wings and the devil's to
    pay.

There are many who think that this calling of
    ours
Is a path where we stroll through the rarest of
    flowers,
Where the lilies and roses and pansies regale
All the boys who go flying along o'er the rail.
They'd be sadly mistaken if once at my side
I could get them to stand for a fifty-mile ride ;
How they'd tumble about like a colicky pig,
Or a bull in a china shop dancing a jig.

If our engines work smooth and we're running on
    time,
We can nerve-strain relax and in harmony chime
With the noble old steed that is flying along,
As her nozzles play bass, while we warble a song;
But the slightest derangement which grates on
    our ears
Ends abruptly the songs of the best engineers.
For myself, at such times, I'd prefer in the Fall,
To be driving old mules on the " raging canawl."

Brother Everett, your hand ! How the years
    have sped o'er
Since we clasped them together in greeting before!
You have given unmerited praise to my name,

Such as only yourself could with modesty claim.
In your "Land that Lies Starward" your Muse
    on her wing
Told us all how she quaffed of the Helicon spring.
May she ever be found soaring grandly along,
To enoble mankind with her Heaven-sent song.

Now my pipe is extinguished, the daylight is gone,
And the brakes of my fancy are set, every one :
There remain but a very few hours till I'll hear
The rich brogue of the caller saluting my ear.
He's the boy who can knock every fanciful flight
Of my noddle up higher than Gilderoy's kite,
As he grunts and he growls like the half-famished
    roar
Of a wolf, in the gray of the dawn, at my door.

MINERS' WAGES ADVANCED.

To Hon. Samuel Sloan, President Delaware, Lackawanna and
Western Railroad.

Your Honor : 'Tis presumption's self
    That urged me from my humble sphere,
To take my old harp from the shelf,
    And sing this strain to catch your ear.

When I perused the joyful news
  That thrilled through ev'ry miner's breast,
I said : " Sam Sloan will ne'er refuse
  My humble thanks among the rest."

Thank God the panic days are past !
  The ten-per-cent. cut-downs are o'er,
And better times are here at last,
  To bless our patient hearts once more.
Indeed it was a welcome sight,
  To read the preface of my song,
It told that dark misfortune's night,
  Now brings a brighter dawn along.

I know you have an honest heart,
  And all your boys here know the same ;
We know you take a poor man's part,
  And think it neither crime nor shame.
We meekly bowed to each decree,
  And gave it our obedient will,
That came in panic troubles free,
  Performing all our duties still.

We watched you stem the darkling tide,
  With anxious eyes we scann'd the stocks,
And cheered you as we saw you guide
  Your roads secure through Wall Street rocks,

Without the loss of spar or sail,
  The skillful pilot that you are,
To weather each financial gale,
  Till Morris and Essex stood at par.

No sooner is the conflict o'er,
  No sooner did good times begin,
Than to each hardy miner's door
  You stole, surprising all within;
Their honest sounds of heartfelt prayer,
  Will be in heavenly mansions stored,
To greet your sure arrival there,
  When called away to your reward.

And now my task is nearly done,
  Back to oblivion's depths I'll fly,
And there concealed I'll try to shun
  Your piercing, shrewd, official eye;
Yet, ere I go, my Muse prevails
  To have me say before we part:
"However fortune tips the scales,
  You'll always have a human heart."

Indeed there is no use at all,
  To please the rude, discordant jade,
Because that fact is known to all
  Your employes of ev'ry grade;

And with your hardy mining band,
　We'll yet be heard in loud acclaim,
O'er hill and dale throughout the land,
　Invoking blessings on your name.

———

TO "HANDY ANDY."

"Handy Andy," since Sam Lover
　Gave the character to fame,
Whom we all admire in fiction,
　And from whom you filched your name,
Every subsequent aspirant
　Seems to blunder more and more
Than the noted Handy Andy
　Did, in Lover's days of yore.

You have published me a liar,
　And have held me up to view,
As a railer at St. Peter,
　And my pious pastor, too.
But his Saintship knows I'm human,
　And will overlook a joke;
For like all light-hearted fellows,
　He enjoys a social smoke.

And to think I'd jibe my pastor!
　Oh, you sanctimonious rogue,
How you moralize just like him,
　In a rich, melodious brogue;
Pointing out the path to Heaven
　For poor penitents to climb;
While yourself may sin and slander
　In a sermonizing rhyme.

If you sat with me on Sundays,
　In a rear located pew,
With the pulpit and the preacher,
　And the people in full view,
Noting those who come to worship,
　Clad in fashion's rich array,
You would surely whisper, "Shandy,
　Very few come here to pray."

Note that lady dressed in satin,
　See how pleasing she can smile;
How her gorgeous plumes are dancing,
　As she sweeps adown the aisle.
Do you think her thoughts are upward
　Where the meek of heart reside?
If you do I'll differ with you,
　For I know she's full of pride.

See the fashionable broadcloth
   Of that portly-looking gent;
Whom I never knew to labor
   For an honest-earned cent.
Do you think the good St. Peter
   Will throw Heaven's gates ajar
To admit him, after taking
   Poor men's dimes across his bar?

See the cushions made of velvet,
   Where they sit and take their ease,
While we poor, less favored mortals,
   On rough boards must bend our knees.
Hear how eloquent the preacher
   Thunders Scripture at the Jews!
As he smiles upon the Gentiles,
   In the velvet-cushioned pews.

Oh, no, Andy; I'm no railer,
   And I don't deny my creed;
But I criticise those preachers,
   Who on choicest fare may feed;
Who ignore the poor and lowly,
   While the rich may favors count.
'Twasn't thus the Galilean
   Promulgated from the Mount.

Have you ever ran an engine
  When the wintry winds did roar,
When the snow, in avalanches,
  Piled against the furnace door ?
When the two old pumps were frozen,
  And the works a mass of ice ?
If you have, don't fear the preachers,
  For you're sure of Paradise.

Have you ever felt the burning
  Of the sun, in hot July,
When the cab would suffocate you,
  And you really thought you'd die ?
If you have, you need not worry
  Much on what the preachers tell,
For, dear Andy, I assure you,
  It exceeds the heat of hell.

Now, my bouchal, in conclusion,
  Let me whisper in your ear :
"In the great unknown hereafter,
  We'll be better off than here ;
While some Scriptural expounders,
  Whom we very often meet,
Will require the polar regions
  To allay their burning heat."

YOU ARE ALL THAT MY FANCY CAN WISH FOR, MY DEAR.

You are all that my fancy can wish for, my dear;
    You're a bright little goddess of beauty;
But a trifle too proud in your notions, I fear,
    And a slave to the strict line of duty.
If you'd banish those prudish opinions you hold,
    And upon my devotion take pity,
Sure I'd prize you far more than full coffers of
    gold,
    And I'd worship your charms, dear Kittie.

You are yet in your teens, so am I, my dear love,
    Or perhaps I'm a year or two older;
Let us sip of those sweets Heaven sent from above,
    Ere the years make our passions grow colder;
We can nobly defy all the trials of life,
    While our hearts are as buoyant as feather;
For with youth, health, and hope, and yourself
    for my wife,
    We will share joy and sorrow together.

Let your lips meet with mine till our souls shall
    unite,
    Do not frown at my loving advances;
But be human, and pledge your affection to-night,
    Let my heart read its doom in your glances.

Ah! I see you respond to me, darling, that smile
  Is a silent, though certain consent, dear, .
For it comes from your heart that's untrammeled
    by guile,
  Oh! I hope you shall never repent, dear.

———

EIGHTY-THREE, FAREWELL.

Farewell, a long farewell, old friend!
  The time is drawing near,
When all our intercourse shall end;
  I tell you, with a tear.
Old Time, that drives with rapid pace
  O'er earthly hills and dales,
Shall quickly hide your wrinkled face
  Beneath our snow-clad vales.

And yet, before you do depart
  Into the great unknown,
To-night I'll ope to you my heart,
  As here we sit alone;
For you have been, in many ways,
  A true and faithful friend,
Whom I'll revere, until my days
  Of fleeting life shall end.

The very moment of your birth
  I heralded with joy ;
And peans rang o'er all the earth,
  To greet the graceful boy.
You then were in your swaddling-clothes,
  A youth of promise fair,
A messenger of love to those
  Who suffered grief and care.

For plenty smiled all o'er the land,
  The wheels of traffic ran
With steady speed, on every hand,
  To bless the toiling man ;
The wolf of hunger, 'mongst the poor,
  Relaxed his deadly hold ;
The merchant felt his risk secure
  Accumulating gold.

My Brothers of the mystic ring,
  Whose countersign is B,
Shall mourn you as a much-loved king,
  Dear Eighteen Eighty-three.
Because throughout your reign we found
  Good friends with voice and pen,
And, for the same, kind thanks resound
  From fifteen thousand men.

From Manitoba's fruitful soil
  To tropical Brazil,
We found reward for honest toil,
  And friends are with us still.
From far Pacific's golden sands,
  Each man who leads a train,
Extends congratulating hands
  To Brothers o'er in Maine.

I fain would have the horoscope
  Of your successor read,
But, ere his eyes on earth shall ope,
  You'll join the legions dead.
We'll mourn you with a doleful tear,
  To speed your parting soul,
And then to greet the young New Year,
  The joyous bells shall toll.

Upon your patriarchal brow,
  I note a sombre cloud;
Poor friend! your hours are numbered now,
  You'll soon be in your shroud.
Perhaps amid a much-loved few,
  Who've reached the mystic shore,
I'll hold communion yet with you,
  Where parting is no more.

17

And if our worldly ways are there
    A social bowl we'll drain,
Of nectar or some vinous rare
    And sparkling as champagne.
Amid the perfume gales that blow
    Round some celestial vine,
We'll chat of scenes we loved below,
    In days of Auld Lang Syne.

Expounders of the Scriptures say
    Eternal joys await
All those on earth who fast and pray,
    To reach the guarded gate,
Where ransomed souls shall enter in
    To homes of endless love;
If so, I'll purge my soul of sin,
    So we shall meet above.

At last the parting hour has come,
    I'll grasp your palsied hand;
With arms reversed and muffled drum,
    Your predecessors stand;
They'll take you hence beyond the skies,
    I hear the tolling bell,
As I repeat, with tearful eyes,
    Dear Eighty-three, farewell.

COME MY LOVE, WITH RAVEN TRESSES.

Come, my love, with raven tresses,
　　Here and sit beside me now ;
Come and give me sweet caresses,
　　While the ringlets from your brow
I will brush with touches tender,
　　'Till I see your face aglow,
In the flush of joyous splendor,
　　Like the happy long ago !

Ah ! the years we've left behind us
　　Have been fraught with care and strife ;
Yet they served to closely bind us
　　On the rugged road of life ;
For our hearts have never faltered,
　　Nor our love diminished cold ;
Though our features may have altered,
　　And the years have made us old.

We are drifting sure and steady
　　To the great unknown beyond ;
But when summoned we'll be ready,
　　We'll resignedly respond.
Dismal death can have no terrors
　　For an angel such as you ;
And your soul, devoid of errors,
　　Shall have mine shown mercy too.

A HAPPY NEW YEAR.

Hear the bells as they ring pealing out on the
    night;
From their clear, brazen throats issue sounds of
    delight;
Through the portals of time there's a stranger
    who comes,
'Mid the blare of loud trumpets and beating of
    drums.
Let us give him a right royal welcome, and sing
Out hozannas to God, for this juvenile King.
Let us all emphasize the old greeting sincere,
And exclaim full of meaning : " A Happy New
    Year ! "

'Tis a custom enjoyed in all civilized lands
To go out making calls and take friends by the
    hands
At the birth of the year, 'mongst the rich and the
    poor,
I have ordered my chariot 'round to the door.
Hear my Pegasus neigh ! He's impatient to fly !
I am mounted at last and away through the sky !
At the speed I am going I'll rapidly near
A few friends, whom I'll greet with a Happy New
    Year.

I see Cleveland beneath. Down, my Pegasus,
    down !

I have got a few friends to salute in this town.

P. M. Arthur, your hand! Dash the clouds from
    your brow,

For I'm not going back to my *darlings* just now.

Till I pay my regards. Here's your hearty good
    health!

May your coffers keep full to o'erflowing with
    wealth—

Do not mind the decanter, it makes me feel queer—

Most sincerely I wish you a Happy New Year.

T. S. Ingraham's next. Here's his latch-string
    outside,

I will enter. Good morning. I've had quite a ride.

I am here with an honest intention to take

Firm grasp of your hand for a friendly old shake.

Please convey to J. H. S. my kindest regards,

And just say that "Dead Beats" are not found
    among bards.

Ere I leave let me trumpet-tone into your ear:

From my heart's depths I wish you a Happy New
    Year.

Now, my noble old steed, to your mettle once more,

Till we make a short call on a far distant shore.

There are mountains below, if my longitude's
    right;

Yes, the Rockies are here, on this crag I'll alight,

Till I find G. D. Folsom. A man who can sit

In a car and delight us with learning and wit :
Ah, he's found amid nature's sublimity here.
Brother Folsom I wish you a Happy New Year.

Oh ! I'd like to go farther ; but see how the sun
Is outstripping my steed, that's enjoying the fun.
Every place where we call he drinks down to the
    dregs.
By the aid of his wings he now steadies his legs.
How I'd love Californian wonders to see !
And the almond-eyed, rat-eating heathen Chinee !
But, my boys, though I cannot partake of your
    cheer,
Take the will for the deed, and a Happy New Year.

Now I'm off to the South, where I'd gladly remain,
For the flight of my steed is distracting my brain.
How the cities appear and dissolve into space !
Here is Dixie below ; I will slacken my pace,
And alight. O, my boys, I'm delighted to say
That there's joy in my heart to behold you to-day !
Please dilute that red liquid, pour lightly, I fear
I've indulged rather freely. A Happy New Year.

Bear me back to the East, while my senses remain,
'Mid the joys of to-day there are echoes of pain.
Brother Everett, the best of good wishes I bring
To your grief-stricken home, where old Death
    left a sting.

l expected to meet you at Buff.?lo, but heard
Of the speedy recall which our meeting deferred.
Now, my worthy old friend, whom I'll always
  revere,
May your grief be allayed by a Happy New Year.

Up and off to the shores of Lake Erie to greet
A few boys of Fifteen, ere our rounds are complete.
Here's a wide-open door, uninvited I'll call.
What a joyful surprise ! Pleasant evening to all !
See how Callahan smiles as he pours out the wine—
Brother Forestall, please put cold water in mine—
Hank Glendenning, your health ! Let us drink
  with a cheer
For the boys of Fifteen on this Happy New Year.

"Handy Andy," acushla ! I'll have to repent
For my feasting to-day, and do fasting next Lent.
You'll excuse me, I hope, I'm as "full as a tick."
And I've thrown for awhile, all my cares to Old
  Nick.
Please uncork a fresh bottle, it's contents we'll
  drain.
Fill our glasses once more full of fancy's cham-
  pagne !
'Tis the "stirrup cup," Andy, ere homeward I
  steer,
Which I drink as I wish you a Happy New Year.

Now for home. It is time to be stretched on the
    bed.
There's the devil's tattoo drumming round in my
    head!
If my steed wasn't jaded I'd ride through the sky
Wishing Happy New Year till the Fourth of July.
As I entered my cot at Ontario's shore,
Here's the brief salutation I got at the door :
" There's no need of me wishing you pleasure, my
    dear,
For I see you've been having a Happy New Year."

TO MY BLACKTHORN CANES.

(PRESENTED BY MR. C. B. BENSON.)

You are welcome, gladly welcome,
    And my heart is in a flame,
As I grasp you, meditating
    On the land from whence you came.
On that Island in the ocean,
    Where Atlantic fiercely roars,
With a never-ceasing fury,
    On its weather-beaten shores.

What an eloquent description
    Of that Island in the sea,
I have heard from him who brought you
    From its verdant hills to me!

With a tourist's eye he noted
  How old Nature's lavish hand
Spread the richest scenes of verdure
  In poor Paddy's native land.

You're a gnarled looking stranger,
  But you're welcome just the same;
And, "my kippeen of shelalah"
  You are not unknown to fame;
For at patterns, fairs and races,
  I have heard of you before,
Where the "peelers" fled before you,
  Or lay sprawling in their gore.

Where coercion acts are yearly
  Manufactured to enslave
The aspiring thoughts of Paddy,
  If for freedom he should crave;
Where the right to carry arms
  For protection is denied,
'Tis no wonder that Shelalahs
  Are so noted far and wide.

You are now among the Yankees,
  Where a man who toils for bread,
If he's sober, just and honest,
  Can erectly hold his head,

And be peer among his neighbors,
    For no titled hordes have we
To debase us worse than cattle,
    As they do beyond the sea.

So, my "splinter of shelalah,"
    And my two blackthorn canes,
You'll be kept amid my treasures,
    While a throb of life remains.
For the sake of him who brought you
    From old Ireland's rebel glades
You are all sincerely welcome
    To my daily promenades.

NUDIS VERBIS.

To Wm. B. Phelps, Oswego, N. Y.

On a feverish night I unconsciously strayed
    Into one of my troublesome dreams,
When I fancied I saw, in his grave clothes ar-
        rayed,
    My old friend, by the sun's setting beams.
As an earnest spectator I stood 'mid the crowd
    Of deep mourners, dejected and dreary,
Where were chanted in accents of anguish aloud,
    The grave strains of the sad Miserere.

Soon the churchman arose, with a sanctified look,
  To bestow the last rites on the dead,
And the service laid down for his guide in the
    book,
  He most fervent and feelingly read ;
At its close he selected a text and essayed
  To mechanic'ly handle his theme ;
'Twas the standard formula church parliaments
    made,
  And I murmured dissent in my dream.

'Twas " From ashes to ashes and dust unto dust,
What the Lord gives he surely will take ;
In divine revelation we'll earnestly trust,
  And be faithful on earth for His sake.
Now we'll tenderly place the remains in the tomb,
  ·Till the arch-angel's trump from the sky—"
"Stand ye back !" I exclaimed, as I sprang from
    the gloom,
  With the tears rolling down from each eye.

"Stand ye back, let me say a few words that are
    not
  On your glib, orthodoxical chart ;
Let me preach o'er the dead, on this grief-stricken
    spot,
  In the eloquent lore of the heart ;
For I've known him and felt the kind grasp of his
    hand,

As it gave me a magnetic thrill,
Like the touch of a holy seer's magical wand,
    And its pressure is lingering still.

"There he lies with the life-tide congealed in his
        veins,
    For his spirit has vanished away,
And his heart that could throb for humanity's
        pains,
    Is now cold in its casket of clay.
I have known him to steal like a thief in the night,
    With good cheer loaded down, to some door,
Where he'd quickly transform into thankful de-
        light
    The complaints of the luckless and poor.

He ne'er paused to inquire of what country or
        creed
    Was the man whom he took to his heart,
But he hugged him up close with a miserly greed,
'   Nevermore from its shrine to depart.
Oh, he looked not to find geographical lines,
    He was deaf to sectarian rules,
As he mingled with friends beyond narrow con-
        fines,
    Of the bigoted, cynical schools.

He was human, and erred in those trivial things,
    To which men who are human incline;

Now, let all of you here who are faultless, spread
    wings,
    And fly off from this earth, you're divine;
Ah! I see you remain, which is proof that my
    dead
    Benefactor had virtues so bright,
That have ransomed his soul, as it heavenward
    fled,
    Into mansions of endless delight.

"Brilliant flashes of wit instantaneously ran
    Through these lips that are sealed evermore;
Such a mind has been rarely bestowed upon man,
    Full of choice chronological lore.
How his forefathers conquer'd or gloriously died,
    As they fought for their country and right,
In the days when men's souls were most stren-
    uously tried,
    Gave my friend patriotic delight.

"Systematic and strict were his dealings with all,
    But his laws were with justice applied;
If we erred and atoned he'd the balance let fall
    To the humane and merciful side.
Ah! he ruled us with kindness and treated us
    here
    As his equals, and not as his slaves.
We shall weep for him hourly, in anguish sincere,
    Till we follow him into our graves."

As I ceased, came a wail of response from the
crowd,
  A most heart-rending, ear-piercing scream,
It arose like the belching of thunder, aloud,
  And awakened me out of my dream.
'Twas a glad transformation from grief to delight
  As the vision of death fled in gloom,
To behold my old friend looking hearty and bright
  Whom I fancied was laid in the tomb !

THE EXILES.

They sat by the camp-fire, their day's toil was
over.
  The song and the chorus went merrily round ;
And yet an observer could plainly discover
  That they were all exiles whose songs did
  abound ;
They sang in full chorus grand anthems delighted,
  Their memories wander'd to scenes far away ;
With hearts full of love their devotion they
plighted
  To Erin, their mother, those exiles so gay.

They thought of the scenes where in boyhood they
sported,
  The mountains, the meadows, the rivers, the
  plains,

The fields where for pleasure they often resorted,
Were fondly remember'd in soul-stirring strains;
Fond hope in each bosom was joyously springing,
  Each face was aglow with remembrances
  bright,
As back o'er the ocean their fancies went winging
  To all their young frolicsome scenes of delight.

All true to the flag of Columbia, dearly
  They loved to behold it's bright folds in the
  breeze;
But there,, in a bond of true brotherhood yearly,
  They sang of the old land far over the seas;
They pledged her their heart's deepest ties of affec-
  tion,
  While life would remain they would faithfully
  be;
They hoped ev'ry link in her chain of subjection
  Would soon from her limbs be knocked off and
  she free.

TWO PICTURES.

When wintry winds in fury beat
  The habitations of the poor,
And stride along on nimble feet
  To many an unprotected door;

Oh, then, the suffering ones within
   Have agonizing ills to bear,
As huddled round, in clothing thin,
   They drink the dregs of dark despair

Convenient to the poor man's shed
   A stately palace rises high;
Its smallest stone, if sold for bread,
   Would make the wolf of hunger fly.
Its fountains flash in brilliant jets,
   From beams of massive chandeliers;
No wonder that its lord forgets
   The bitter wail of human tears.

His lady fair can hourly ride
   In furs and robes of costly price;
And on the frozen streets may glide,
   In festive mirth, 'mid snow and ice.
Her days move on in joy serene,
   Her nights amid the ball-room's glare ·
She's paid the homage of a queen,
   By those who circle round her there.

The splendor of her equipage
   Outrivals eastern chariots old;
Her prancing steeds are all the rage,
   Their trappings decked with virgin gold.

Her lap-dog has more tender care
   Than thousands of God's lowly poor!
"Tis fed upon such dainty fare
   As will its brutish tastes allure.

Oh, if she'd only pause and think,
   How much distress her wealth could save
Amongst the crowds that starving sink
   Down into many a nameless grave;
Perhaps upon life's tragic stage,
   A Christian part she'd oftener play;
The tears of grief she could assuage,
   And drive much discontent away.

See yonder child, her feet are bare,
   Her half-clad body shakes with cold;
The snow flakes kiss her tangled hair,
   More golden than the purest gold.
Alas! she weeps for parents dead.
   She seeks from passers-by relief;
A penny or a crust of bread
   Would dull the pangs of childish grief.

Poor waif upon life's stormy sea!
   Too soon your ill-starr'd youth shall fade,
There's no relief or sympathy
   From costly silks and rich brocade.

18

In hearts like ours the echoes lie,
   Which spring to life in accents wild,
Whene'er we hear the doleful cry
   Ascend from poor misfortune's child !

Down, pen ! more skillful hands than mine
   Must wrestle with man's grievous wrongs,
And speak inspired from every line,
   Instead of rude, discordant songs.
The task—it seems devoid of hope ;
   I fear the poor must drift in gloom,
Until the skies in glory ope,
   To call us hence from out the tomb.

MY LOVE IS A BLOOMING YOUNG MAIDEN.

My love is a blooming young maiden,
   Endowed with a frolicsome mind.
Her eyes are with witcheries laden,
   As ever 'mongst maidens you'll find.
She's gentle, kind-hearted, and loving,
   And says she is faithful to me.
I fear her affections go roving ·
   Too often in frolicsome glee.

One eve in the twilight I caught her
  Up close in my fervid embrace,
And there on my bosom I taught her
  The love of my heart in my face.
She tore herself off and she started
  Away with the speed of the wind;
'Twas thus in the gloaming we parted,
  And lonely I linger'd behind.

The next time we met 1 demurely
  Sat listening to lectures she gave—
Her mother's eyes watched us securely—
  I promised to always behave;
Of course I surrender'd discreetly;
  What better just then could I do?
Because I was shadow'd completely,
  Right there with her mother in view.

The clock told the hour of leave-taking.
  Young Flora strolled out in the porch,
Her sides full of laughter were shaking,
  And I like a deacon at church,
Until we were clear of the prying
  Her mother directed along;
Again I embraced her, defying
  The eyes that were watching for wrong.

My kisses profusely were given
   On lips luscious ripe to be pressed;
I there had a foretaste of Heaven,
   As I pretty Flora caressed.
When off from the gaze of her mother,
   She gave all her feelings full play,
And, ere with affection we'd smother,
   We tore ourselves slowly away.

—————

MY FIREMAN.

There he sits with a smile on his black, smoky face,
   And a droll-looking glance in his eye,
As he notes how the "pointer" keeps up in its
     place,
   As our noble old steed seems to fly.
He's the happiest man to be found on the train,
   For I promised I'd write him a song,
To the air of that musical, pious refrain:
   " And we'll Roll the Old Chariot along."

Yes, I'll write him a rhyme; 'tis the least I can do
   For a lad whom I really admire,
And, besides, my dear reader, he's one of the few
   Who can closely attend to his fire.

He imagines he has a fine, musical ear,
　　Though he can't tell a march from a jig;
And his voice, which he fancies melodiously clear,
　　Has a trill like the grunt of a pig.

But aside from his musical talents, he knows
　　He is gifted in ways I despise;
All the men on the trains are our deadliest foes,
　　Just because he's the father of lies;
And many a time in the cab when we've found
　　A full share of annoyance and grief,
A train man or two we'd see prowling around,
　　To berate the uncrucified thief.

If it's tallow or waste we're in need of he'll seek
　　Out the place where they hide their supplies,
And will pilfer sufficient to last us a week,
　　Right from under the baggage-man's eyes.
There is scarcely a trip that we make but I'm
　　　starved,
　　For I never yet knew him to fail
In selecting the tid-bits, all seasoned and carved,
Which I carry for lunch in my pail.

He shall soon change his seat right across to the
　　　place
　　Where the wrinkles shall furrow his brow,

And the deep lines of thought shall be marked on
    his face,
  That looks beardless and boyish just now.
All his monkeyish tricks shall be brought to a
    close,
  For when once he's promoted he'll find
That he'll need all his thoughts for protection of
    those
Who are riding in coaches behind.

———

AN EPISTLE TO A FRIEND.

Dear Friend : The time is opportune,
This evening in delightful June,
To spend a pleasant hour with you,
Whom I admire in friendship true.
The Moon is floating like a queen ;
In azure skies she moves serene ;
All nature is in silent mood,
No sound upon my ears intrude.
I upward turn my eager eyes
To penetrate the silent skies ;
But, Jim, Alas ! my sluggish brain
Can't comprehend the starry train
That move along through upper air,
Nor see the power that keeps them there.

But this I know : agnostics may
Proclaim their creed till dooms dread day,
And yet, in spite of all they say,
There is a being who can sway
This universe, and who can trace
The track of all that move in space,
Can guide them and direct them still,
To move according to His will.
What puny things we mortals be,
Mere insects tossed upon life's sea,
And yet, we often times incline
To doubt there is a power divine.
Sure all created things we view
Proclaim a great Creator too.
I'm of your faith and can agree
Convinced by sights I daily see.
Opposed to each contracted creed,
Where conscience never can be freed
From narrow bounds, from bigots' sneers,
From hypocritic scoffs and jeers.
Your faith is mine, 'tis grand and broad,
"Through nature up to nature's God"
We worship, with the silent heart,
And eyes which see our God impart
His mercies here to all mankind,
With our full strength of heart and mind.
A few more years at best will tell

The whereabouts of Heaven and Hell;
If all we heard since glorious youth
From preachers' lips are words of truth,
Or simply planned to make us feel
The thrust of wiley churchmens' steel.
I think the last, and Jim, I know,
Like me you scoff eternal woe.
My eyes are loaded down with sleep,
I'll into bed this instant creep,
I'll sermonize no more to-night,
But mail you this at morning's light.

DEDICATION LINES.

READ AT ROCHESTER, N. Y., BEFORE THE MEMBERS OF DIVISION
18, B. OF L. E.

To dedicate this splendid hall
    To friendship, and each mystic rite,
Is why we've gathered, one and all,
    Who are assembled here to-night.
The brave and fair are in accord,
    With smiles and cheers to speed you on,
And 'round your sumptuous festive board
    You wear the laurels you have won.

When man shall toil for fellow man
   To aid him in his hour of need,
He fills the great Jehovah's plan,
   And proves a brother true, indeed ;
'Tis such you've proved who in this hall
   Are circled round in modest mien,
And we are honored by the call
   To join the members of Eighteen.

At this baptismal font we see
   Paternal sponsors standing round,
Who always will our guardians be
   While justice in our laws abound ;
They're honored men, your city's pride,
   Whom you have made by vote and voice,
I see them here on every side,
   Distinguished as the people's choice.

From Manitoba to Peru,
   From San Francisco o'er to Maine,
We're sure to find our brothers true
   To duty's call on every train ;
And friends spring up to help us on—
   They've done it oft and will again—
Because our Order rests upon
   Approval of our fellow-men.

And, brothers, here's our worthy Chief,
    Who truly fills Jehovah's plan,
In every sense, 'tis my belief,
    That Arthur is an honest man.
For ten long years his counsels wise
    Have led us safely on our way,
Until our strength and growth surprise
    Our best and dearest friends to-day.

Well done, Eighteen! tho' but a part
    And parcel of the mighty whole,
Your acts shall thrill each brother's heart,
    Where'er he be between each pole.
The widows' and the orphans' prayers
    Ascend like incense to the skies,
To guard and keep you from the snares
    Of envious men's detracting lies.

No dynamiters here are we,
    Nor enemies to social laws;
Our Brotherhood shall foremost be
    In every good and worthy cause.
We'll upward build, no shameful brawl
    Shall ever mar our path of right,
As proof, behold this splendid hall
    We're dedicating here to-night!

IT IS BETTER TO SING.

It is better to sing of good frolic and fun,
    And to whistle all care to the wind, boys.
Than to sit and repine and all merriment shun,
    With a brake set on heart and on mind, boys.
To the devil we'll fling ev'ry pulse throb of pain
    That keeps beating confined in our breasts, boys.
Yes, we'll burst every link of the sorrowful chain,
    Which we nurture right under our vests, boys.

'Tother evening young Flora came tripping along,
    With her tresses afloat in the breeze, boys.
Sure she captured my heart with her musical
    song,
    And she made me soon feel at my ease, boys.
Oh! I gazed in her eyes lit with honor and love,
    And I felt as courageous as Mars, boys.
Although I'm as gentle and kind as a dove,
    For her sake I could march to the wars, boys.

I was sad ere we met, but her beautiful hand,
    Which she placed in my big, brawny fist, boys,
Made me joyous as any one found in the land;
    For its thrill I could never resist, boys.
So you see there is no use in nurturing grief,
    And hugging it close to your heart, boys.
Better win some young Flora to give you relief,
    Then the blues will all quickly depart, boys.

TO THE OFFICERS AND MEMBERS

OF THE LADIES' SOCIETY OF THE BROTHERHOOD OF LOCOMOTIVE
ENGINEERS, BURLINGTON, IA.

While we live we'll hear of wonders,
  I suppose they'll never cease,
For with each succeeding season
  They all rapidly increase;
But the latest startling wonder
  That salutes our listening ears,
Is a pioneer Division
  Of our lady engineers!

I'm delighted, full of rapture,
  Yes, and rigmarolling fire,
For I see there's no profession
  To which woman can't aspire.
Now we find her at the throttle,
  Let us hail her with a cheer;
Let each brother send a greeting
  To each sister engineer.

I extend you all a welcome,
  You shall find I have the grip,
And the mystic salutation,
  Which we plant upon the lip.
It was rather dry embracing
  Through the long years past and gone,

But henceforth we'll use the lip signs
   With our sisters every one.

'Tis surprising to me, ladies,
   How you ever clasped the throat
Of our roystering, rambunctious,
   Rampant, rollicking old goat.
I confess the night I rode him,
   He was in a roaring rage,
But perhaps his pranks are cooling,
   Like all human goats, with age.

Well, you're in, and you are welcome
   As the flowers that bloom in May,
And I know 'tis woman's nature
   Amongst social lads to stay;
We will treat you as our equals,
   For you've nobly paid your fees,
And we'll let you take our places
   When o'erworked and needing ease.

Heretofore men did the running,
   Now the husband·trips may change
With the wife, who'll take his engine,
   On a plan they'll both arrange;
He'll stay home and mind the babies,
   'Twill be penance for his sins,

If, like me, he's blessed with squallers,
  In the shape of healthy twins.

He can pack, key up, set wedges,
  And do all the oiling round,
Ere the engine leaves the station,
  So she'll take her safe and sound ;
. Then, as off you're booming, ladies,
  Watch each house when passing by,
And perhaps some other darling
  Of your husband you may spy.

She will think he's on the engine,
  And may gently wave her hand
To salute him when he's passing,
  With a sign he'll understand ;
If your nature should be jealous,
  And you meditate a crime,
Should you stop the train to kill her,
  You'll be pulled for losing time.

And when back you come with vengeance
  Bubbling up at every breath,
Give the lad you left dry-nursing,
  Time to pray before his death.
You are sure to think he's guilty,
  And will have your own sweet way,

Yet, before the lamb is slaughtered,
  Let him have a chance to pray.

Keep your temper with your fireman,
  For you'll often need his aid,
But avoid the gay conductor,
  Be you widow, wife or maid;
If you don't you'll live to rue it
  With a sad, remorseful mind,
For I know some sly old devils
  'Mongst the tinselled caps behind.

I will be your guardian angel,
  And protect you from the snares
Of those oily-tongued deceivers,
  With their sweet, seductive airs;
I'll applaud your undertakings
  With a hearty voice and pen,
And, before the year is over,
  You may hear from me again.

THE RIVER ST. LAWRENCE.

Oh! you grandly rolling river
  That majestically rides
On your pathway to the ocean,
  Bearing on the countless tides,

From the mighty lakes above you,
    With an undiminished force,
Since old Time first sent you bounding
    On your never-ceasing course.

You have filled my heart with rapture,
    As I gazed in speechless awe
At the noble works of Nature,
    Which within your bounds I saw
At the loveliness profusely
    Scattered over many miles;
Where the Master-hand triumphant
    Decked the famous Thousand Isles.

Here is foliage surpassing
    All the tints and rainbow dies,
Which the sun in mid-day splendor,
    Grandly paints from azure skies;
We find shade and sunshine blended,
    Em'rald green and burnished gold;
Making up a vision splendid
    And surprising to behold!

How transparent are your waters!
    There the angler's vision tells
Where the finny tribe are sporting
    In the rocky rifts and dells;

There with hook and line delighted,
  In his birchen-tree canoe,
He may sport amid the treasures
  Which are lying 'neath his view.

Hear the strains of music rising!
  See the stately steamers ride,
With their happy group of tourists
  On its clear, translucent tide;
Mark the yachts whose safe manœuvres
  Keep them clear of countless oars,
Which are sending liquid di'monds
  Rippling onward to your shores!

When the queen of night is reigning,
  With her starry train above,
It is then all hearts commingle
  In the bonds of fervent love;
From your depths they are reflected,
  Just as peaceful as the smiles,
Which the angels lavish fondly,
  To salute thee, Thousand Isles.

Oh! Great Being, omnipresent,
  Teach our hearts to render praise
For the blessings which You send us,
  Lead us all to know Your ways;

19

And when life on earth is over,
　Let our souls to You arise,
From such scenes as here I'm viewing,
　To our home beyond the skies.

MOONLIGHT FANCIES.

Pass your pipe along, partner, and here
　You and I'll have a sociable smoke,
For the evening is balmy and clear,
　And fair Luna's forgotten her cloak;
Through the deep azure hue of the sky,
　She triumphantly rides like a queen,
And she looks with a ravishing eye
　Fondly down on all nature serene.

Such a night how I love to recall
　The dear scenes of our youth up to view,
When we fancied life's highway was all
　A delightful parade for us two;
Ere the trials and battles began
　To be fought for the bread which we eat;
When each yearned to march as a man,
　With the crowds who were thronging the
　　street.

Then, how slowly the weeks seemed to roll,
  And old Time seemed a laggard, whose feet
Would ne'er lead to the coveted goal
  Where fruition of dreams we would meet;
Now, we're awed at the progress he made
  O'er the years like a meteor's flight,
And oh, friend! how I sigh for the glade
  Where we sported in boyhood, to-night.

What a fanciful picture we drew
  Of a future remote from us then,
Of the paths which we both should pursue,
  When we'd march to the music of men.
We were sure of success on the road,
  And we dreamt not of hopeless defeat;
All unheeding we joyfully strode,
  Ever futureward fortune to meet.

When 'twas wealth we aspired to—sit down,
  And don't jump from my side in disdain—
For there is not a pauper in town
  Has more right than myself to complain;
When 'twas love—see that mouthful of smoke;
  Note how quickly it faded in air;
'Twas an emblem of Cupid's sweet yoke,
  When we browsed on the lips of the fair.

How we thirsted for fame, and we prayed
　　For the time when we'd march with a gun
Did you find it the day that you made
　　Such a race for the rear at Bull Run?
Or the day you ran old Ninety-Four
　　Through the flock of fat gobblers and saw
The old farmer, who furiously swore
　　That he'd shoot you according to law.

Well, we've all got a mission to fill;
　　There's no changing Jehovah's decree;
And the terminal station is still
　　In the distance for you, friend, and me.
Let us faithfully run through the strife,
　　Till the trip of our lives shall be o'er,
Till old Death shuts the throttle of life,
　　And sets brakes on eternity's shore.

————

THE EXILE'S RETURN.

The wharf-lines off are quickly cast,
And we are outward bound at last.
The skies are fair, the tide is free;
Our course is to the open sea.
Our voyage, happily begun,
Points eastward to the rising sun;
Where boyhood's scenes, long years gone by,

Attract us, and we backward hie,
    To have a brief sojourn.
And now, to each remember'd place,
Fond mem'ry dearly loved to trace ;
Where flowers bloom the year around,
And health in ev'ry breeze is found,
    The exile's steps return.

Our noble steamship cleaves her way
With steady speed through ocean's spray ;
Each revolution of her wheel
Vibrates along her noble keel,
Which stood the crash of mountain seas,
And many a chilly wintry breeze.
She bears us on, our hopes and fears,
The dreams of many toilsome years
    Will soon be realized.
Old Erin's hills once more to view,
Arising from the waters blue ;
Again to step upon her soil,
And for a season flee from toil,
    Are wishes dearly prized.

Perhaps some callous heart may sneer
At all those tender feelings dear,
Which cluster 'round our early days
And merit more than passing praise ;

Which rise with every heaving breath,
To bear fruition ere our death;
A steady wish, once more to view
Those bye-gone scenes of roseate hue,
  Which fancy can beguile.
Where first a father's love we felt,
Or at a mother's knee we knelt,
And learned to lisp the simple prayer,
For God to guard our lives from care,
  In Erin's sainted isle.

The man whose noble heart can feel
The glorious sports of boyhood steal
In through the cares of riper years,
Until his eyes o'erflow with tears,
Can judge the joy of him whose hopes
Are cluster'd 'round the sunny slopes
Of cloudless youth, life's morning prime,
When backward to his native clime
  He goes in middle age;
Expecting everything the same,
As when he felt youth's joyous flame,
Amid companions, blithe as e'er,
Defied the touch of cruel care
  To mar life's opening page.

The liberated clouds of steam
Above the funnels brightly gleam;

The engines groan with toiling stroke,
And backward trail dense banks of smoke.
The log-book tells of rapid strides
We daily make o'er ocean tides;
It tells we near the wished for shore,
From which we sailed long years before,
   Across the Western main.
And now, like pilgrims to a shrine,
We swiftly move through trackless brine.
Before another sun shall fade,
A landing may be safely made
   On Erin's shores again.

Behold beneath the morning skies
A glorious scene of grandeur rise!
Oh, joyous sight! Oft wished for day,
For which the exile's heart did pray;
Through thirty hoary winters long,
We sighed for you in prayers and song,
And now our eyes are bless'd at last,
Dear Erin we are nearing fast
   Before a pleasant gale!
Our decks present a moving mass
Of anxious people as we pass
By chalky cliffs and em'rald hills,
A rapture through each bosom thrills,
   When nearing old Kinsale!

Upon our beam we sight Tramore,
And soon our voyage shall be o'er.
Our feet shall touch the sainted sod,
Where humble hearts salute their God,
At every rising of the sun,
And when his course is westward run.
Dunleary ! after many years,
Again we shed pathetic tears,
        Unchecked they slowly fall ;
For moments such as these we sighed,
When moving 'mid the ceaseless tide
Of busy men, who throng the plains,
Where priceless Freedom truly reigns,
        Impartially for all.

But where are those we hoped to find ?
The comrades dear we left behind ?
The loved companions of our youth,
Whose hearts were filled with hope and truth ;
Who played with us on primrose banks,
Long, long ago, in boyish pranks,
When fleet of foot, and light of heart,
We studied neither grace nor art
        Upon the village green ;
But true to nature, whiled away
The hours, until the sun's last ray
Had faded o'er the flow'ry plain,

Or sunk beneath the heaving main?
     They're nowhere to be seen.

The very houses, once so tall,
Appear diminutive, and all
The things we conned in mem'ry o'er,
Are lost to view for evermore.
The daisies seem to be less fair
Than when we wove bright garlands there
Long years ago, the birds, whose song
Did through our yearning fancies throng,
     Discordantly we hear.
All things have changed. The churchyard
  where
A mound was scatter'd here and there,
Is now a mass of simple stones,
Where lie entombed the mold'ring bones
     Of those we loved so dear.

Oh, hopes we cherished, daily prized,
Expecting they'd be realized.
Alas! our sighs and tears were vain
When hugging each delusive train,
Which longing fancies fondly wove
Around the scenes of early love.
The gulf dividing youth and age,
O'er which a weary pilgrimage
     Reluctantly was made,

Can ne'er be crossed, how e'er we crave
To bridge it o'er this side the grave;
Its depths contain the buried joys,
Entombed since we were careless boys,
   And froliced in the glade.

The sunny slopes, and winding streams,
Oft visited in countless dreams;
The wooded hills, the teeming plain,
O'er which we viewed the waving grain;
The mossy dells, the leafy grove,
Where we in early years did rove;
The river clear, which swept along,
The birds we heard in ceaseless song,
   Have all so sadly changed!
They never more will look the same
As when we felt the glowing flame
Of happy childhood, long ago,
Because our eyes are dimm'd with woe,
   And hearts with care estranged.

TRIALS AND TRIBULATIONS.

An attack of malaria which lasted a week,
Had a wholesome effect, as I now am quite weak,
 And altho' convalescing, yet sad;
Oh! I thought: is the battle of life with its ills

To be finished at last amid fevers and chills,
   Ere the spirit ascends to its God ?

When the pulse of the heart's running rapidly
   high,
And a lack-lustre glance indicates in the eye,
   That 'tis time to prepare for the worst,
What a long chain of ills will parade in full view,
Every one looming up with a sulphurous hue,
   Which our own selfish bosoms have nursed.

As we gaze with the unclouded eye of the mind,
Over scenes which we thought were forgotten
   behind,
   How we shiver and shake with dismay.
In our health 'twas our boast the good times we
   enjoyed,
But in illness we find the illusion destroyed,
   And for pardon most humbly we pray.

When old Death hovers nigh how the conscience
   can sting,
As the spirit prepares far away to take wing
   From the casket which bore it in life.
But the Lord only knows on what course it will
   fly,
Whether up in a joyous career to the sky,
   Or go down to contention and strife.

How my thoughts travel'd back with a yearning
    *delight
To the springtime of life when the future looked
    bright,
    As I gazed down the vista of years ;
Then I never once dreamed as the future did ope
To my view from the top of youth's mountain of
    hope,
    That the distance held valleys of tears.

In such rapid succession the seasons sped on,
Very soon the bright visions of youth were all
    gone,
    Nevermore to enliven the scene.
I have found, as so many discovered before,
That the thorns lie thick on each path we explore,
    On the mountains, and valleys between.

How we murmur about our disconsolate lot,
In a rancorous mood, just because we have not
    An abundance of this world's wealth ;
If we'd pause, and reflect, in our hearts we would
    prize,
As the best of all gifts sent us down from the
    skies,
    The enjoyment of bodily health.

Ask a man on his bed when he's tortured with
    pain,

If his thoughts are distracted by miserly gain.
　If his answer be "yes" then we know
That he'll order a pocket put into his shroud,
So he'll carry his hoardings away from earth's
　　crowd,
　To the place he's expecting to go.

What a fool!　All the wealth that was ever
　　concealed
In the bowels of earth to his soul wouldn't yield
　Half a second of peaceful repose;
Little use will he have for his ducats when Death
Lifts the scales to blow off all his miserly breath,
　Ere the clay rattles down on his nose.

There are many who'll laugh at the tone of my
　　song,
Who imagine their lives are devoid of all wrong,
　And their acts can pass muster on high;
Let them once get a chill which shall shake them
　　all o'er,
From the roots of their hair to their heart's in-
　　most core,
　And then truly confess what they'll spy.

It will make us content with what fortune may
　　send,
And when life's checkered voyage approaches its
　　end,

If we're poor we can think ourselves blest;
We are sure to be placed just as deep in the clay
As the men who bequeath all their millions away,
  And can go more contented to rest.

AT THE GRAVE OF AN INFANT.

The mother's heart is sear'd with woe,
  Her dearest hope is fled;
The tears in torrents downward flow,
  Her first-born boy is dead.
The friends who gather 'round the sod
  Would fain assuage her grief;
But she alone must look to God,
  To give her heart relief.

A few short moons he nestled near
  Her kind, maternal breast,
Where, twined around her heart-strings dear,
  She'd lull him off to rest;
She'd closely scan his infant face,
  As in her arms he'd lie,
And ev'ry want she'd quickly trace,
  Beneath her watchful eye.

Like flowers, chilled with frosty air,
　He wilted in his bloom ;
And now, behold him lifeless there,
　Above his childish tomb.
The mother's tears are rolling free
　Upon the casket lid,
But in a moment more he'll be
　From human eyesight hid.

Ah ! yes, strew flowers on his grave,
　All you with senses calm ;
But for the mother's grief I crave
　Some sympathizing balm ;
A tempest rages in her breast,
　Her hopes are 'neath the sod ;
She'll never more find tearless rest,
　Till with her babe and God.

TO THE MEMBERS OF DIVISION NO. 136.

A REPLY TO COMPLIMENTARY RESOLUTIONS SENT TO THE AUTHOR, ON RECEIPT OF HIS PHOTO.

I have always had faith that the future would
　bring
A few gifts from Miss Fortune to help me along,
How the jade at my ear did delusively sing
　Of her plans for my welfare, in soul-stirring
　song.

But, alas! like the paymaster's car on some roads,
  When I thought her at hand, from my grasp
    she would slip.
Yet, she'd feed me with smiles, which were silver-
    gilt goads,
  And she'd stuff me with hopes just as worthless
    as scrip.
She is coming again from some boys in the west,
  And she's singing a song most delusively sweet,
Telling how they're uniting to "feather my nest,"
  For a trip to old Erin with outfit complete.
Oh, the joy of my heart is unbounded to-night.
  'Tis a fact and not " blarney " I'm giving you
    now,
For there's nothing can give me one-half the de-
    light
  As a European voyage, salt billows to plow.

How I yearn to view the green fields of my birth !
  I would like to see Paddy, as found in his home,
Till I'd note him, tho' shackled, all bubbling with
    mirth,
  Which he never forgets in the climes where
    he'll roam ;
Save a renegade few, whom all mankind despise,
  Who'd deny their old mother, and spit in her
    face.
How they struggle their accent and names to dis-
    guise,

Though the map of the island is stamped on each
    face!

We have Charlies from Kerry, and Williams
    from Clare,
  We have Delias from Carlow, and Jules from
    Athlone,
We have Raymonds from Wicklow and Hanks
    from Kildare,
  And we've red-headed Celias just out from Ty-
    rone!

By the Gods! I aver they were Biddies and Pats,
  In the land where potatoes must pass for a
    feast,
Where their honest old fathers first christened
    the brats,
  With the aid of some patriot, God fearing-
    priest.

Oh, I love the old land, tho' in shackles she pines,
  And I dream of the valleys, each river and rill,
To be found dotted over the verdant confines
  Of her borders, where freedom is sought after
    still.

May each renegade wretch with a sand-papered
    tongue,
  When it wags to deny her with scoff and with
    sneer,
Be cut off from communion all mankind among,
  Till some sheriff persuasively tickles his ear.

20

I will bring every member of One-Thirty-Six
    A decoction of blarney out fresh from the stone ;
But, my boys, if I judge by your roystering tricks,
    You have got a sufficiency now of your own.
I see Cavner is out with a Quixotic plan
    For the good of the boys, which I very much fear
Will not work, till we're sure of perfection in man,
    Or until the much-looked for Millenium's here.

The old ship of the Brotherhood's booming along,
    With her bunting all set to prosperity's gales ;
Don't you think, Brother Cavner, the act would
      be wrong,
    Should we alter her course or the set of her sails?
There's no sign of a tempest on weather or lee,
    Not a pirate's on board that we know of to-day;
So my boy, let her float gayly over the sea,
    As she's steering at present in glorious array.

To you all my regards. Keep my face to the wall
    When the wives of some Mormon are visiting
      'round.
'Tis a fashion of ladies to visit each hall
    Where a handsome collection of boys may be
    found.
There's but one wife allowed to each man in New
    York,

And the man who wants more must be proof
  against fire;
As for me, I must keep pretty steady at work
  For the lady who's wedded to Shandy Maguire.

———

A WEDDING PRESENT TO J. T. K.

I suppose it is my duty
  A few compliments to pay
To the bride and groom together
  On their glorious wedding day ;
I will do it, but I'm doubtful
  If this rhyme will suit your ear,
Yet, we ofttimes have to listen
  To some truths we hate to hear.

A few months ago I dragged you
  From the tomb of one 1 knew
To be upright, true and faithful,
  During twenty years, to you.
And I pitied you sincerely,
  For I truly thought you'd rave
Everlastingly about her,
  Till you'd join her in the grave.

You put crape upon your engine,
    And you wore it on your hat,
And you looked like Misery's mother,
    As within the cab you sat;
Then, I thought you grieved sincerely,
    Now, I know it was a plan
You invented, so the ladies
    Would know where to seek a man.

And one found you, Jerry, darling.
    She's a simple little fool,
That's but lately out of short-clothes,
    And had better be at school,
Than to wed a man whose whiskers
    Are kept dyed from chin to ears,
To conceal the grizzled tell-tales
    Of his forty-seven years.

"Sure an old fool is the worst fool,"
    As my mother often said,
And I've always known her, Jerry,
    To have wisdom in her head.
Folks will take her for your daughter
    Promenading at your side,
Till some wag will kindly tell them :
    "It is Jerry's bouncing bride."

I have been surmising lately
  There was "something in the air,"
With your laundried linen daily,
  And your oily head of hair,
As you'd go to pull a coal train,
  Scarcely noting passers by,
With your nose at such an angle,
  That it pointed to the sky.

You would sport a cane on Sunday,
  As you went to see your love,
And each greasy hand was hidden
  In an over-crowded glove;
And you tried to look as boyish
  And as youthful as your son;
But, you old, deluded driv'ler,
  We were laughing at the fun.

Man, when in the "roaring forties"
  Going down the grade of life,
Has a soft spot in his noddle,
  When he wants a second wife;
He is sure to seek a young one,
  For some reason of his own,
And he needs her just as badly
  As a hungry dog a stone.

You will soon need porous plasters
　　Pasted all along your spine,
And you'll take a nervous palsy,
　　And you'll have a quick decline,
And you'll need a pair of crutches,
　　And a doctor, and a nurse,
And perhaps your bouncing beauty
　　May be wanting a divorce.

She'll soon tie your toes together
　　With a half a yard of tape,
And upon your nickle door-knob,
　　She shall hang a bunch of crape;
And she'll stand beside your coffin
　　Shedding glad tears on your face,
Thinking on what youthful lover
　　She shall marry in your place.

My dear, married, lady-readers,
　　There's a moral to my song,
Which you've found if you have closely
　　Scanned its truthful lines along;
You have all got "Jeremiahs"
　　Who're impatient for the time
When old Death shall send you booming
　　Up to some celestial clime.

I advise you most sincerely
    To be careful of your health,
You will find it pay you better
    Than accumulating wealth,
For some second wife to squander
    On her captivating charms,
Once your husband has her snoring
    In his old, delighted arms.

TO A FRIEND.

I have just got the news of your marriage,
    Indeed, 'twas a pleasing surprise,
Sent from one who would always disparage
    The brilliancy beaming from eyes
Which are lit by the loves and the graces,
    Bewitchingly dancing in joy ;
And could laugh at all maidenly faces
    That sought to ensnare you, my boy.

You've been caught in the soft, silken netting,
    Which Cupid around you entwined ;
Yes, and all your past sermons forgetting,
    You entered the bondage resigned.

I suppose you took leave of all others
  You lavished affection upon ?
For in marriage, you know, like our mothers,
  We're only entitled to one.

Now, adieu to the nights which we sported
  Around the convivial board ;
Where a few social fellows resorted,
  With minds full of merriment stored.
Where we lingered from night until morning,
  Carousing in story and song ;
Till old Sol would peep in to give warning
  'Twas time to be moving along.

I suppose all the keepsakes, and tokens,
  And trophies of love you possess,
From the girls which you said were heart-broken,
  You returned to console their distress ?
If you havn't, make haste, boy, and do it,
  'Twill make your path smoother through life,
Or if not, time will come when you'll rue it,
  If ever they're found by your wife.

When we meet in the future, demurely
  We'll talk like two deacons in prayer ;
With a drawl to protect us securely
  Against our dear wives' critic stare.

They will think we were saints ere we met them,
    They'll fancy that each won a prize,
And imagine us anxious to get them—
    But, boy, we'll throw dust in their eyes.

All our old, glorious evenings are over,
    We'll simply salute and pass on ;
We'll no longer wade knee-deep in clover,
    Our nights of carousing are gone.
We will sigh when we think of the chorus
    We raised from a union of throats ;
Hereafter, dear boy, we've before us
    A very rich crop of " wild oats."

If I ever meet Fanny, I'll tell her
    Her charms are on the decline ;
And I'll ask what misfortune befell her
    Her chances on you to resign ;
And if Susie, or Nellie, or Mollie,
    Remember your light-spoken vows,
I will say you repent of your folly,
    And wish you had each for a spouse.

Now, I'll do a friend's share in consoling
    The darlings you parted in grief ;
For, like you, I've a knack at condoling
    With maidens to give them relief ;

Yet, I don't think they'll die broken-hearted,
  Because you are married and gone ;
They know many a maid you deserted,
  Before you struck colors to one.

———

AWAY WITH YOUR FLIMSY ROMANCES.

Away with your flimsy romances,
  All you who sit dreaming of love ;
In wedlock you take many chances,
  When tied to your conjugal dove.
The one to please me must be mistress
  Of wholesome, culinary art,
And move through my sensitive stomach
  Right into the joys of my heart.

Bright eyes may be pleasant to gaze on,
  And lips may be lusciously sweet,
They'll please you, perhaps, for a season,
  Until you need something to eat ;
But when all your vitals are gnawing
  For dishes more solid than air,
The smiles of the darling won't stifle
  The stings of your appetite there.

If she can preside in the kitchen,
    With other accomplishments too,
Why, then, you may call her an angel,
    Whom Heaven conferred upon you.
I'd never complain of her features,
    Tho' coarse every lineament be,
But call her the fairest of creatures,
    Who feeds me on good things at tea.

Or when from the bed in the morning
    To breakfast I'm told to arise,
To see her the table adorning,
'   Can give me most joyful surprise.
The smell of rich coffee's enticing,
    The toil of the day it beguiles,
I start to my duty rejoicing,
    And kiss her good-bye full of smiles.

"All beauty's skin deep" says the proverb,
    And liable quickly to fade,
Remember it well when your choosing
    Some artful, young, exquisite maid;
Be sure she can cook a good dinner,
    For, mind you, when beauty is gone,
'Twill save you being damned as a sinner,
    To know such a prize you have won.

TO A REPORTER.

WHO COMPLIMENTED A CONDUCTOR.

Ah! say you so, Mr. Reporter?
   Indeed, it is wonderful news!
And really, I think 'tis a subject
   Quite worthy an hour with my Muse;
For I've known Tom for years, and I've pulled him
   A many a mile, off and on,
And I like to partake of the pleasure
   Men feel when their work is well done.

It is pleasing to see in your paper
   A name that's as worthy as his,
And your readers will all be delighted
   To witness the smile on his phiz;
And yourself—but of course it is fancy
   Which runs through my ignorant brain—
When I say for that "puff" you'll be welcome
   To ride when you choose on his train.

To the bright, sparkling eyes of the ladies
   A hero he's certain to pose;
He's all smiles, like a cat in the cupboard,
   With dishes of cream at her nose.
How the darlings admire his white linen,
   His di'monds, his watch-chain, and rings,
Oh, they'd think him an angel off duty,
   Except that he's minus the wings.

How the furrows of care are now creeping
   Unbidden his features about;
They are there from the torture he suffers
   Each day that his coaches go out.
The suspense of his calling is fearful!
   The strain on his nerves is severe!
And the cushions in coaches are thorny
   To sit on in comfort, I fear.

When the nights are dark, foggy, or rainy,
   Torpedoes may fail to explode,
And the train may be suddenly halted
   At stations not marked on the road;
For his eyes, ever watchful of danger,
   Can see far ahead in the night,
But he'll soon make the passengers happy
   By telling them things are all right.

When the pumps will not work how he worries.
   And often injectors will " break; "
It is sad at such times how he'll suffer;
   In mental affliction he'll shake.
When the pointer goes back, or when bearings
   From friction are smoking and hot,
'Tis a pitiful sight to behold him
   Bewail his responsible lot!

With the mercury down below zero,
   And chilled from his head to his toes,
One would think that he'd die from exposure,
   As icicles hung from his nose;
In the drawing-room car is no comfort
   For Tom, when the snow-drifts are high,
But the boys in the cab are in clover,
   When Boreas shrieks wild through the sky.

At a halt, or a jar, or a movement,
   Which comes unexpected, he'll frown;
And sharp words in profusion he'll mutter,
   Regarding his blue-shirted clown;
Oh, how wise then the passengers think him,
   When fears he'll create to allay,
For they know his cool head will protect them
   From obstacles strewn in the way!

I could sit here a week eulogizing
   His curly, executive head,
But a voice is discordantly jarring
   The strings of my lyre from the bed;
And the stars in the eastward are fading
   Away from the track of the sun,
So dear Mr. Reporter, good-morning,
   All further temptation I'll shun.

COME, FILL UP YOUR GLASS TO O'ERFLOWING.

Come, fill up your glass to o'erflowing,
   And drink to the time when we met;
When hearts were with merriment glowing,
   In days we're too apt to forget,
When you and I followed our fancies,
   Regardless of where we would stray,
Providing sweet lilies and pansies
   Were blooming along by the way.

We sipped of the sweets which were growing
   On lips luscious ripe to be pressed.
We fondled the dear ones, well knowing
   The pleasure they'd feel when caressed.
Now fill! Here's to Susie and Mollie
   We loved long ago in their teens;
Who always felt social and jolly,
   And acted as graceful as queens.

Bethink you the night in the gloaming,
   When sweet airy-nothings we wove,
To please the young maids who were roaming
   Beside us in Mayberry's grove?
Come, drain off a bumper to Fannie,
   . The darling who strolled at my side,
And I will fill up to dear Annie,
   Who laughed when you called her your bride.

Once more let us fill while we've reason,
    And Mem'ry presides on her throne;
Our hearts can feel joy for a season,
    When thinking of days that are gone.
We've care to contend with too often,
    When breasting the billows of strife,
So, here's to the thoughts which can soften
    The buffets we meet with in life.

Too soon will enjoyment be over,
    And full every line on the page;
We'll live the remainder in clover,
    And laugh in the teeth of old Age.
With wine we can drive away wrinkles.
    Now, fill up our glasses once more;
We'll not care for Time when he sprinkles
    Our locks with gray hair from his store.

TO J. D. HAMMOND.

What a tramp you have had through the realms
    of thought!
    How the corns must torture your feet!
And what byways and hidden resorts you have
    sought
    Through the years that have vanished so fleet!
I had almost forgotten the days you recall

From your memory's plentiful store,
Light your dudeen, avick ! till we'll chat over all
Those bright days that we'll never see more.

Nearly twenty long years since the night that
we made
Our debut on the stage to the throng!
Oh, how quickly old Time is descending life's
grade,
As he drags us reluctant along.
How we fancied that night what great actors we
were,
And we looked for bouquets at the close,
But, alas ! save a cabbage head flung at us there,
No applause from spectators arose.

How you made up your phiz for a villainous part,
And how tragic you strode o'er the spot
Where you fancied the people would thrill at the
art
You displayed jibing "Judy O'Trot."
But, my boy, by the smoke that ascends 'round
my nose,
She soon brought all your antics to grief
With the handy shillalah, concealed 'neath her
clothes,
As she hunted you off like a thief.

Sure poor "Flaherty" never was fit for a priest,
Holy church does not want such as he ;

21

For he never could fast, but the first at a feast
 Was the same sly, seductive Magee.
And old "Judy" is now a plump matron, whose
 waist
 Is as round as a hillock of hay !
And yourself—an old bachelor, stuffed up with
 paste,
 Which you use to drive wrinkles away.
" Ragged Pat " is still here puffing mouthfuls of
 smoke,
 Doing pennance in fevers and chills,
For the days and the nights that he scoffed at
 life's yoke,
 And derided humanity's ills.
He is changed, I confess, and I fear for the worse,
 Growing old with the buffets of time ;
Oh, I truly believe he inherits the curse
 Meted out to all garblers of rhyme.
Dennis Hayes he is rich and respected besides ;
 " Slang," he lives, but a warning to all
Who would dare follow woman, with serpentine
 strides,
 'For they surely will meet with a fall.
So, take warning, my boy, and go get you a wife,
 You are yet a good looking gossoon ;
Find some old woman's daughter to sweeten your
 life
 With a dose of " chin music," aroon !

" Gentle Florence " is sleeping the sleep of the
    dead,
    Where Ontario's clear, liquid wave
Rolls along on the beach, in monotonous tread,
    And besprinkles the grass on her grave.
And " Old Stone " has been judged by the Ruler
    of kings,
    At the throne of Jehovah on high ;
Let us hope he's an angel, adorned with wings,
    'Mongst the Christ-ransomed souls in the sky.

How the memories afloat, clad in ghostly array,
    Intermingled with smoke, as I write !
Let us fill a fresh pipe till we drive them away
    To the graves of oblivion to-night.
In a few fleeting years at the most we will be
    Their companions again evermore,
For we soon will be launched on that limitless sea,
    Which no mortal did ever explore.

LITTLE BROWN EYES.

Here's my little brown-eyed beauty,
    With her head of sunny curls.
She's the sweetest, and the dearest
    Of all darling little girls.

She comes laughing when I call her,
  And she'll jump into my arms,
Where I gaze in silent rapture
  On her early budding charms.

If I'm sad her ringing laughter
  Soon dispels the gloom away,
For her genial disposition
  Can change night to glorious day ;
She is ever kind, and willing,
  And obliging as can be ;
She is all my earthly treasure
  With her carols full of glee.

With paternal feelings, tender,
  I bestow each pure embrace,
Till she's nearly suffocated,
  As I spread them o'er her face.
May the years pass lightly o'er her,
  And the future have in store
Every virtue to endow her,
  Till her days of life are o'er.

TO "HANDY ANDY."

Handy Andy, what a spalpeen
  Is your mother's darling son,
And how droll you cut your capers
  When you're dealing out your fun.
You're a first-class bastinado
  In the manner which you write,
And a moralizing rascal,
  Who pursues me day and night.

How you gloat about my torture,
  When I'm shaking with the chills,
In the rhymes you keep prescribing,
  That can gripe me worse than pills.
You are acting as a mirror
  Holding up before my view,
Sins of which I know I'm guiltless,
  Can I say the same for you?

If you look within your bosom,
  If you'll pull aside the veil
Which conceals your imperfections,
  And repeat to us the tale
Of all horrors you'll discern,
  Through the years you left behind,
What a moral I will scribble
  As a warning for mankind!

You will find the ten commandments
  Are all knocked in smithereens;
All our holy church's precepts
  You destroyed when in your teens;
For pride, avarice, and envy,
  Anger, gluttony, and sloth,
Are all sins of your commission,
  I will take my honest oath.

You would like to tell me, Andy,
  How to lead a better life;
While yourself would play the rascal
  With your neighbor's handsome wife.
But, beware! the day of reck'ning
  Has a story to reveal
Of your midnight capers, Andy,
  That you never can conceal.

All the fishes in the ocean,
  Served on Fridays and through Lent,
Will not purge away your follies,
  In your efforts to repent.
You will need a scourging penance,
  Like all hypocritic rogues,
Some sharp carpet-tacks well scattered
  In a pair of cowhide brogues.

I am not much of a Christian,
    And I'll tell the reason why:
In my youth I suffered, Andy,
    'Neath my good old mother's eye.
I was doomed for holy orders,
    Where I'd lead a saintly life,
'Till the faculty determined
    I had better take a wife.

So I'm here in toil and trouble;
    And hereafter, who can tell
Whether up I'll go to Heaven,
    Or go down below to—Well,
It don't matter where they'll send me,
    I'll be found good souls among,
Where I'll hear your cries below me,
    Asking ice to cool your tongue.

DOCTOR LAWRENCE REYNOLDS.

(Delivered at the Benefit Entertainment, June 15, 1882.)

Kind friends, assembled here to-night,
    Whose gen'rous hearts beat high and warm
For him removed away from sight,
    With hoary locks and aged form;

Who struggles 'neath a stranger sky,
  A mere subsistence there to find;
Your presence here can testify
  To numerous friends he left behind.

The lengthened shadows of his life
  Are stretching into evening gloom;
No kindred near, no child, no wife,
  To smooth his pathway to the tomb.
But we who've known his better days,
  When friendship seemed to smile secure,
Will ne'er refuse him well-won praise,
  Who now is lonely, old and poor.

His creed is simple; it is laid
  Upon the universal plan
That Christ upon the Mount portrayed
  When dealing with his fellow-man.
His heart is pure and free from guile,
  His views are broad and unconfined;
He scorns alike the bigot's wile
  And all the unbelieving kind.

With pathos, mirth, and heart-felt song,
  He wages ceaseless war on might;
He never yet upheld a wrong,
  But always advocated right.

For this he's exiled from the shores
   Where first he drew his native breath;
For this he fought in Union wars
   Where Treason met its bloody death.

Meagher's Brigade can testify
   On many fields, how hard he strove
To keep forever floating high
   The banner, which all freeman love.
Beneath the green flag in the van,
   He faced the battle's cloudy marge,
Where blood in crimson rivers ran,
   Which marked the valiant Irish charge.

He never asked the creed or clime
   Of dying men upon the sod;
But preached to all that text sublime,—
   To trust a universal God.
If human aid their lives could save,
   He'd labor there to ease their pain;
If not, the pathway to the grave
   He'd smooth for every hero slain.

And such a creed as that will bind
   The good and true of every land;
And such a man will always find
   Staunch friends to take him by the hand;

Misfortune's bitter gales may blow
   And strike such men with icy breath,
But friendship's grasp will ne'er let go
   Till eyes are closed and sealed in death.

Oh! had I but his gift of song,
   And were his genius mine, I'd write
How well I thank the generous throng
   Of friends, who love him here to-night.
Tho' absent we shall ne'er forget
   How well he filled old Nature's plan;
And till his sun of life shall set,
   We'll aid the old and lonely man.

LINES READ AT A UNION MEETING, BANGOR, ME.

Now, my brothers, imagine me standing before
   you,
   In talent, the least of our Brotherhood's bards.
I have made (in my mind) this long trip to encore
   you,
   As here you've assembled, and pay my regards.
I have left the cold hills of New York, where the
   waters
   Are frozen for months in a vast, icy plain;

Took a tramp, as it were, to the wives and the
    daughters,
    And husbands and Brothers, residing in Maine.

Sure, methinks I see Tucker, that prince of good
    fellows,
    Who always is certain of Brotherhood cheers,
Because he is kind, as his actions all tell us,
    And treats with respect all his loved engineers.
May his name sound along down the ages in
    gladness,
    Enshrined in the hearts of the good and the
    brave,
'Till old Death whistles brakes, and we place him
    in sadness,
    To rest, as our tears we bestrew on his grave.

We brought Foss—he's our Chief, and a kind of
    a dandy,
    His trips are all made with his gloves on his
    hands.
How I'd like to write down just the same of poor
    Shandy,
    Whose fists are both greasy from scouring
    the glands.
Brothers Angel and Spier, Keith, Towle, Lowe,
    and Sampson,
    Rowe, Richardson, Sweet, Ferry, Gilbert and
    Dean,

Every one of them worthy a nobleman's ransom,
  And faithful as any existing in Maine.

And we've Fortier here too; yes, and Coburn
    smiling,
  And Davis, and hearty, good-natured "old
    Dan,"
Close, and Rafter, in mirth and the moments
    beguiling,
  With stories of numerous miles which they ran.
Brothers Hilborn, Gilpin, and Cobb are delighted,
  And taking a little respite from rough toil;
I will mention one more who came near being
    slighted,
  You know I refer to my countryman, Doyle.

To the rest of you here, though denied of the
    pleasure
  Of saying I know you and met you before,
I will whisper my joy, the first moment of leisure,
  And talk in the language of mystical lore.
Oh! I know there is pride in each social reunion,
  To tell it defying the power of my pen,
As we gather in crowds and converse in commun-
    ion,
  Uniting in friendship all Brotherhood men.

Tho' in Bangor we meet we are banded together,
  Cemented by ties which are dear to each heart;

And we come, disregarding the distance or
  weather,
  I know with regrets from your town we'll de-
    part.
But while mem'ry survives we will think of this
  meeting,
  And shrine up the moments we spent at your
    side,
Till assembled again for another such greeting,
  Some day, not far off, as we futureward glide.

While we're true to the cause we'll be true to each
  other,
  And men will respect us all over the land;
Let us prove there is more in the title of "brother,"
  Than simply the name and a clasp of the hand;
If we do, Payson Tuckers all over the nation
  Will surely befriend us when needing their aid;
For each one can be faithful, tho' lowly in station,
  And truthful and honest, while climbing life's
    grade.

WINSOME JENNIE.

Winsome Jennie came to-day
  With a wreath of smiles to meet me;
As she spied me, when at play,
  And with radient joy did greet me.

Childish curls hanging down
　　O'er her neck, such sunny tresses!
Not a sign of fear or frown,
　　Dealing out her sweet caresses.

Jennie, little can you tell
　　Of the years long since departed,
When your mother was a belle,
　　And I nearly broken-hearted!
How the times have changed since then!
　　Here I'm now in mid-years, rather
Wrinkled, like all toiling men,
　　Old enough to be your father!

I can see your mother's eyes
　　Sparkling in unconscious gladness!
But, they cost me many sighs!
Yes, and nights of sleepless madness,
　　In the dreamy long ago!
Ere the cup of youth flowed over,
　　And exposed its dregs of woe,
To her old time ardent lover!

How my youthful fancies wove
　　Garlands out of airy notions!
How I'd rhyme of dove and love,
　　Pledging all my heart's devotions!

Daily, hourly. Could it last?
  Well, it didn't, for we parted,
When our dream of love was past
  Neither one died broken-hearted!

When we meet so seldom now,
  She is like some saintly sister;
And denies each loving vow
  Which she made as oft I kissed her.
I am changed I must confess,
  She has lost her former graces.
Silver streaks through ev'ry tress;
  Turkey tracks on both our faces!

Handsome blonde! I see her yet,
  As in dreams I backward wander!
When she swore to ne'er forget,
  But through life to love the fonder.
Lovers' oaths! A perjured train,
  Retrospectively are dancing,
In each settled, sober brain,
  Of those moments spent entrancing!

Now, at last, our dreams are over,
  And your fickle-hearted mother
Went to browse in other clover,
  Like myself she wed another.

Winsome Jennie! never tell
    Of this resurrected story,
For, you know, my little belle,
    Both our heads are growing hoary.

TO GRAND CHAPLAIN EVERETT.

You are now the Grand Chaplain of Brotherhood
    men
  And, by virtue of office, the "Sisterhood" too,
Will peruse with delight every flash of your pen,
  And think them infallible coming from you.
There's a license attached to your calling we
    know,
You are sure of a welcome wherever you go.
'Tis a roving commission to steer where you
    choose,
Just as free as the flights you partake with your
    muse.
For a man with a clerical cut to his coat,
Will be sure of distinction and worthy of note.
'Tis a calling I love from the depths of my heart;
They're the boys who can furnish us compass and
    chart
For a flesh-purging trip, on the ocean of life;
  Where we're told to avoid all contention and
    strife,

And admonished to scourge the grim tempter
    away
That has made his abode in our caskets of clay.
We are told to give alms, practice fasting and
    prayer,
Whilst themselves can sit down to rich, sumptu-
    ous fare.
Yes, they mark out the course they insist we must
    steer,
    For the portals of Heaven, where bliss evermore
Will be meted out freely to each engineer,
    When he climbs up the grade of the "Beautiful
    Shore."

Now, my worthy old friend, theological schools
    Do not teach all the wisdom this world contains;
For I've known one or two egotistical fools
    Who supposed they were preaching to men
    without brains.
On the fat of the land every day they could dine,
And they gargled their throats with full bumpers
    of wine ;
Dressed in choicest of broadcloth for daily pa-
    rades
As they sauntered, consoling wives, widows and
    maids,
You are not of this class, for I know you of old,
I am sure you will lead all the sheep to the fold.
Like the piper of Hamelin, your musical trills

Are the strains we will follow up Heavenly hills.

All the ladies here praise every song from your
    lyre,

And they say you sing sweeter than Shandy Ma-
    guire,

I supposed myself once the high priest of the
    dears,

Which I was till the darlings became engineers.

But, alas! I'm dethroned, and you reign in my
    place;

  For all clerical chaps with mellifluous gab,

With a smooth, oily tongue, and a meek looking
    face,

  Are more prized by the ladies than men in the
    cab.

Oh, I wish that I'd never made rhymes about
    goats!

  Or betrayed half the secrets our lodge-rooms
    contain,

Or divulged to the "sisters" the way they could
    note

  How their husbands keep flirting when out on
    the train.

Yes, I rhymed about twins, about squallers, and
    brats,

For I hated them worse than the Kilkenny cats.

When a man runs all day he finds little delight

Crawling home to the kids he must dry-nurse at
    night.
These were sorrowful thoughts, they influenced
    my song,
And my pen followed freely the stanzas along,
As I thought of the bottle, the cradle and pair
Of young monkeys, whose lungs could out-bellow
    ᶜ a bear,
Or a master-machinist whose tongue gets untied
When he sees his pet engine come home on one
    side.
When the fruits of our marriage come single
    they'll do,
    And they help to atone for our manifold sins,
But whenever they come in installments of two,
    Heaven pity the wretch who's afflicted with
      twins.

I would like to continue this subject, but Lord!
    How the ear-piercing screams of the imps in my
      ears
Penetrate to my heart, till all writings abhorred,
    And my eyes are a deluge of sorrowful tears.
In conclusion, a little advice I'll bestow:
Shun the ladies the same as your deadliest foe;
Or if not, all the peace of your life they'll destroy,
And your laughter they'll change into weeping,
    my boy.

Be they " Sisterhood Lodges " or " Lady Aid "
    rings,

Individual sirens, or angels with wings.

If you practice these precepts I'm certain you'll
    find

More serenity, comfort, and peace for your mind,

Than be singing for husbands to match with the
    dears,

On a voyage in wedlock where hardship begins,

Where the market with some is controlled by the
    " Bears,"

And with others 'tis " Bulled" by cantankerous
    twins.

———

CHRISTMAS EVE IN CAMP, 1885.

They sat before a genial fire,
Their hearts were kindled with desire.
All trans-atlantic faces there,
And anxious looks each one did wear.
They peered into the growing gloom
The shades of night spread 'round the room,
As if they sought some comrade dear,
And listened for his footsteps near.
At last they heard the welcome sound,
As on the walk it did resound ;
The well-known form, in joyous song,

Came caroling in speed along,
Till in their midst stood Rory Joyce,
The owner of the silvery voice,
   With features all aglow!
He was the spokesman of the band,
He searched for news of fatherland,
Then told it to his comrades dear,
Who caught it in each eager ear,
   This tale of friend and foe :

"Oh! boys," he said, "fill up each glass,
To-night the toast must freely pass ;
I've got some glorious news to tell
About the old land and Parnell ;
He's sweeping obstacles away
From Derry's wall to Bantry Bay ;
From shore to shore, from sea to sea,
He says he'll make old Ireland free.
On every hill the bon-fires blaze,
Like erstwhile in the glorious days,
When noble Brian led his train
Of pikemen after fleeing Dane.
Election's over and he's won,
Without the aid of pike or gun,
   Or shedding precious blood ;
In loyal bonds each man was bound,
And—save one dastard—all were found

Beneath his banner, till the tide
Of battle to our leader's side
      Came rolling in a flood.

"Oh! think of all the hopeless years
We stood our foemen's haughty sneers!
And when we sought redemption, blows
Were given to allay our woes ;
We suffered in our slavish chains,
The most excruciating pains ;
We sought to burst them, but we found
We were more tightly in them bound.
Disunion in our ranks plowed deep ;
Our foemen fruitful crops did reap
Of all the patriotic men,
Who failed to gain some secret glen.
The gallows, block, the rack, the rope,
Have oft extinguished Erin's hope,
      And flooded her with tears ;
But soon again her sons would rise,
And struggle hard to win the prize,
Of freedom from the alien band,
Who terrorized our native land
      For seven hundred years.

"But, boys, the clouds are rolling by—
I see them with prophetic eye—
The sun of freedom's glorious day

Shall soon send forth its genial ray,
Illuminating hill and dale,
From Antrim's heights to old Kinsale.
From Galway's shores to Wicklow's hills,
The sweeping vales and babbling rills,
The plains of choicest em'rald green,
The rivers, gliding on serene,
Each old, historic field and height,
Shall soon enjoy the wished for light,
And Irishmen shall win applause,
By framing just and wholesome laws,
   Where statesmen, eloquent
In all that makes a nation free,
Uniting men fraternally,
And legislating like the days,
When Erin did the world amaze,
   In Grattan's parliament.

"Now fill and drink success to all
Who did obey our leader's call,
And may another Christmas eve
Behold a nation round him weave
Her brightest garlands, may he stand
The liberator of the land."
As Rory ceased each man arose,
And gave three hearty cheers for those
Who made the latest glorious fight,

And showed the world our cause is right,
That union in our ranks at last
Can win success. The ages past
Have proved how brawls can wreak more woe
Within our midst than mail-clad foe,
    Upon the tented field.
And there on old Kentucky's soil,
Those hardy sons of honest toil,
Who loved this land of freedom true,
Rejoiced that Ireland's landlord crew
    Would soon be forced to yield.

A TRIP IN DREAMLAND.

I have mounted to Heaven on pinions of light,
Where St. Peter and I had a confab one night,
Talking over old times with the keenest delight,
    As the stars far beneath us did gleam.
1 have also been down to those regions below,
Which are sadly in need of a blizzard of snow,
Where the souls of the damned are expected to go,
    But my visits were made in a dream.

From a thirty hours' trip t'other evening I sank
For a snooze on the welcome soft side of a plank,
With a big lump of coal which I took from the tank,
    For a pillow to rest my tired head.

I was soon in a dream and with hurricane speed,
On the back of a weird, supernatural steed,
I arrived at a place which looked dismal, indeed,
    Where are kept in confinement the dead.

In an instant a palsy I took in my knees,
And my eyes at an angle of ninety degrees
Began squinting about like a rat stealing cheese,
    And my horse fled away with a moan;
I would give all the wealth I e'er saw to get back,
I'd be happy in snow drifts as high as the stack;
Oh, I suffered the tortures of gibbet or rack,
    When along came my friend Mick Malone.

"By the piper that played before Moses," said
    Mick,
"You are lucky to get from the clutch of ould
    Nick,
And you're welcome, a thousand times welcome,
    a vick!
    To a place in the penitent gang.
Take a seat, Shandy, dear, on this trunk of a
    tree;
I'm delighted to see you, acushla machree!
Light your pipe, take a whiff, and then pass it
    to me,
    For my lips are both blistered with 'whang.'"

"Arrah! Micky," said I, "in the name of the
  Lord,
What's the name of this country I'm in? By
  my word,
'Tis a bleak looking place, and I never yet heard,
  of a region so dismal before.
With a laugh he replied, "Purgatory, my boy,
And as bleak as it looks we have moments of joy
That a board of directors can never destroy,
  In the manner they ground us of yore."

"Do you tell me so, Mick? Faith I've heard of
  the place,
'Tis a clime where poor souls must wipe off
  their disgrace,"
"You are right," said my friend, blowing into
  my face
  A whole mouthful of "Nigger-head" smoke.
"You've a long time to stay, Brother Shandy,"
  he cried.
But your sentence it dates from the moment you
  died,
You were lucky to have the good priest at your
  side
  To redeem you from Ingersoll's yoke."

"Am I dead, Mick" I asked. "As a herring"
  said he,
"Just as sure as you're sitting and talking with
  me."

"Well, if such is the case, I'm delighted to be
    With a comrade I truly admire.
Mick, I prayed for your soul many times since
    the day
That we covered your body 'neath four feet of
    clay,
When I scarcely could drag your poor Jennie
    away,
    And I thought that she, too, would expire."

"Arrah, Shandy, how is my poor Jennie," he
    said,
"Is she happy?" "She is; for, my boy, she is
    wed
To a dashing young gent, who consoles her in-
    stead
    Of a husband she sighed for like you.
Your insurance she got and she dressed up in
    crape;
By the aid of cosmetics and cotton, her shape
Would entice a poor hermit with mouth all agape,
    And the dimes she had plentiful, too."

Mickey said not a word, but his eyes filled with
    tears,
For he knew he was one of those soft engineers
Whose big toes are no sooner turned up on their
    biers
    Than their wives go in search of a "mash."

In the richest of crape on the street they parade,
And they look with disdain on a simpering maid,
For they're posted in tricks of the man-catching
    trade,
    And, besides, they have plenty of cash.

There were numerous crowds of both sexes about,
Occupied in regrets for past actions, no doubt,
Or, perhaps, they were watching a chance to get
    out
    O'er the well guarded walls of the place.
As they sauntered along there were many I knew;
'Mongst the females I saw I remembered a few,
And they all seemed to stare in surprise at me,
    too,
    With a look of delight on each face.

"Can you tell me," I said, speaking gently to
    Mick,
Who kept weeping away at the dastardly trick
Which his widow played on him impatiently quick,
    "Who is that fellow there on the right?"
"He's a playboy," he said, "and Belisle is his
    name,
Not a moment of peace have we had since he came,
He's a noted disturber, and fills us with shame
    At the way he can pick up a fight."

"Who are these fellows here just appearing to
    view?"
"They are Barry and Garland of One-Fifty-Two,
And a pair of sly codgers, between me and you,"
    Said my ghostly old friend with a grin.
"Who is this fellow standing abreast of us now,
With a smile on his broad, intellectual brow?"
Mickey said: "He's the chap who kicked up such
    a row,
    In behalf of our widows, named Lynn."

In a moment or two M. J. Lynn moved along,
Soon I heard a few words of a comical song,
And I noticed Nat Sawyer, who moved with the
    throng,
    By the side of a sweet little dear.
"Who's the lady," I said, who is walking with
    Nat?"
"She's a skating-rink belle, and as spry as a cat,
But old Death came along and he down on her sat,
    And soon Sawyer caught on to her here."

George Van Tassel strolled listlessly by with an
    air
Of the deepest abstraction, akin to despair,
And the "Lives of the Saints" he perused with
    great care,
    As I judged from the look of his face.

Peter Gibson marched next in the scope of my eye,
He was singing a hymn called "The Sweet Bye
and Bye,"
To a band of she-angels, all ready to fly
Far away from his saintly embrace.

"Who's that chap over there with a tear on his
nose,
And a clerical cut to his well fitting clothes?"
"'Tis your friend, Delos Everett," said Mick: I
arose
From my seat in the greatest surprise.
"What's the matter?" he said. "Sure I thought,"
I replied,
"From the manner he preached, that the moment
he died
Heaven's portals would swing to admit him inside,
To eternal reward in the skies."

"Behold Dutcher and Donaldson fronting us
there,"
"Do you tell me so, Mick? Point them out to me.
Where?
Oh, begor! now I see them, a beautiful pair
Of New Yorkers I truly behold!"
"Here comes Ingraham, too, and his sentence is
light,
Very soon he'll be poising his pinions for flight

To a place where good souls enjoy endless delight,
  Over streets paved with ingots of gold."

"Be in order, my Brothers," in thunder tones
    clear,
Came a voice like a dagger-thrust piercing my
    ear.
Oh, I trembled in dread, as the Grand Chief drew
    near,
  With a ponderous gavel of oak.
"By the Lord, Mick, I'm off! let me bid you
    farewell,
For I'd rather be down with the kid gloves in
    —— Tell
Billy Thompson to go for the skating-rink belle,"
  And in anguish of heart I awoke.

――――

ON THE ORGANIZATION OF DIVISION NO. 167.

ORDER OF RAILWAY CONDUCTORS, OSWEGO, N. Y.

On occasions like the present,
  There's a feeling of delight,
Radiating round my goose quill,
  As the stanzas I indite ;
For a grand, new star has risen
  In your galaxy, and I
Have a personal opinion,
  'Tis the brightest in your sky.

They're a band of noble fellows,
    Each one filling nature's plan,
And prepared to take position
    In the Brotherhood of man;   •
Upright, honest, gentlemanly,
    Faithful, steadfast, tried, and true;
Each one handsome as Adonis,
    When arrayed in gold and blue!

I have rode ahead of many,
    During long and tedious years,
And I know they're royal fellows,
    Who admire their engineers;
For their " All aboard " is ready
    When the time arrives to go,
And they cheerfully assist us
    In the sunshine or the snow.

I have known them let our firemen,
    Go and ransack through the train,
When in search of waste and tallow,
    And they never would complain;
For our engines here are limited
    To beggarly supplies;
And when stealing from the trainmen,
    They are sure to shut their eyes.

They have Bibles in their coaches,
  Which they carefully peruse,
They know all about the Gentiles,
  And are posted on the Jews ;
And when female ears are willing,
  How they pour the Scriptures in
To the darling little creatures,
  To avoid committing sin !

I have heard of some conductors
  Who have captivating smiles
To bestow on handsome ladies,
  Riding over many miles,
But I know it is a falsehood
  Calculated to assail
The unblemished reputation
  Of the blue-coats of the rail.

There was never yet an angel
  Half as virtuous in life,
As the boys in this Division,
  Each one faithful to his wife.
There's no Brigam Young amongst them,
  Make a note you sirens all,
When upon their trains you're riding,
  And expecting them to fall.

23

They can take your whole dimensions,
  From your crimson colored nose,
To the neatly turned ankle
  You display in silken hose;
And your perfumed breath in whispers
  Passes powerless through their ears;
They are proof against seduction,
  Try your wiles on engineers.

Now I think I've said sufficient,
  And although 'tis written tame,
I desired to eulogize them
  To the breezy heights of fame;
But my Muse she is a groundling
  That can never upward soar,
Where I'd love to place my heroes
  'Mongst the gallant knights of yore.

* * * * * * * *

I regret not meeting Chapman
  When he made his visit here,
They all vote him a good fellow,
  And I know they are sincere;
But I send him honest greeting
  Ere I drop my weary pen,
Though I'm but a simple unit
  In the brotherhood of men.

A NEGATIVE VOTE ON THE "WOMAN'S DEPARTMENT."

Have a " Woman's Department !" God help us !
  We've too much of petticoat rule ;
We're crushed and caressed by the women,
  'Till each one parades as a fool.
We have heard "womens' rights" from the
    rostrum,
  The pulpit, the press, and the pen,
'Till we cry from our hearts full of anguish,
  " What rights are intended for men ? "

Have a " Woman's Department! " I shudder
  To think how your sex would employ
All the space we would vote you each number,
  The peace of our lives you'd destroy.
You'd be writing of Tom, Dick or Harry,
  And praising the cut of each jib,
'Till we'd all be your slaves, like old Adam,
  From whom you have stolen a rib.

We have now many "Lady Divisions,"
  Where sisterhood grips are the rage,
Where the Brotherhood boys are berated
  As slow for a husband-hood age.
We have "lady-aid" lodges and "circles,"
  And "socials," and lord knows what not.

Do you think for a Woman's Department
　　A space in our *Journal* we've got?

We will vote you some space in our bosoms,
　　And give you a place on our knees,
Where we'll whisper the passwords and tokens
　　Essential to take your degrees;
We will sing you "soft nonsense" in plenty,
　　And keep your eyes dancing with joy;
But a Woman's Department—no, never!
　　I swear by each twin-tortured boy!

Had you sent us a plan or prospectus,
　　Wherein your intentions we'd note,
Perhaps you'd have got the department
　　In spite of my negative vote.
"Oh, acushla machree," said my mother,
　　The night I marched off to be wed,
"If you'll take my advice you'll stay snoring,
　　Alone in your peaceable bed."

Gloomy wisdom of years! sure the poet
　　Conceded he'd mystical lore
When he sang of events which were coming,
　　And casting their shadows before.
Had I heeded the warning she gave me,
　　The crow-feet of care would be light,
And my twins, who excite you to laughter,
　　Would be in oblivion to-night.

You've a musical voice; I'm delighted
  To welcome yourself to our ranks;
You have taken my side against Everett,
  For which I extend you my thanks.
He is trying to march with the ladies,
  Whilst you and I laugh at the fun.
Very soon we will hear an explosion
  Resound from a " breech-loading gun."

In behalf of my Brothers, I thank you,
  Right here, in these lines of my song;
Now the innocent boys may keep flirting
  With women while passing along.
I am glad my suspicions were groundless
  When thinking them guilty of crime,
And their wives will unite with me, madam,
  In lavishing praise on your rhyme.

THE HATS OUR·FATHERS WORE.

Hurrah for Grover Cleveland; he's the leader
    of our band,
The Moses who we long have sought to reach
    the Promised Land,
Where plenty smiles on ev'ry side to bless the
    wond'ring stare
Of those who long have sighed and prayed to
    breathe its purer air.

And, now, we're marching breast to breast, in
    solid, stately tread,

A mighty army on the move, a victor at our
    head.

Such columns of true Democrats were never seen
    before

As here parade beneath the hats our honest
    fathers wore.

Last night Oswego's streets ablaze with thous-
    ands in their pride,

Made sluggish blood course forth anew from
    hearts long sorely tried,

By grim defeat,in former years,but now the times
    are changed,

For Democrats march side by side who have been
    long estranged.

With flambeaus,flares,and oriflammes, with wild,
    hilarious cries,

It seemed that Grover Cleveland's name did pene-
    trate the skies.

Our voices were like breakers on Ontario's rock-
    bound shore,

A mighty host,beneath the hats our noble fathers
    wore.

The very earth resounded with the glory of our
    cause,

Presaging that right soon we'd have more pure
    and wholesome laws,

That plenty would the poor man bless, that thrift
    would rule the land,
That idle wheels again should hum, and thievery
    be banned ;
That men have burst the galling chains which
    fettered them so long,
That Right shall crush the viper head of that
    foul despot Wrong,
That Cleveland will protect each man who'll
    cross Atlantic o'er
To visit Europe 'neath the hats our good old
    fathers wore.

I HAVE ROUGHED IT ALONG.

I have roughed it along o'er the ocean of life,
    And I've passed its equator some time.
'Twas a voyage so far amid turmoil and strife,
    Where the seas rolled in billows sublime !
I was awed by their grandeur, and longed for a
    calm,
    To escape from such vengeance awhile,
Which would give to me courage, a much needed
    balm,
    And illume my sad face with a smile.

Oh ! I love independence, and fain would I fight
    Till I'd gain it and live at my ease ;

Then I'd sing with a free and untrammell'd de-
    light,
    Just such songs as my fancy would please.
If I found out a tyrant, whose purse-bloated heart
    Would be turned far away from the poor,
I would flay him until his two eye-balls would
    start
    From the place where he thinks them secure.

There's a Siren now singing a song at my ear,
    Where she sang it so often before,
And I fain would such soul-stirring melody hear,
    Tho' I live its deceit to deplore ;
Sure she sings me there's land I will shortly enjoy,
    Where the flowers in fragrance bloom,
Where its rightful possessor will not me annoy,
    Once he's called to reside in the tomb.

I will surely inherit my forefathers' soil,
    And it lies underneath the green sod,
Measures two feet by six, the reward of their toil,
    Which they got as they left for their God.
Can a millionaire boast of an iota more,
    When his spirit is summon'd from hence ?
He's no richer at death, tho' his coffers flow o'er,
    Than the man with a few paltry pence.

Mausoleums right over his bones may arise,
    Obelisks may ascend in the air,

Yes and monuments tower aloft in the skies,
  Telling all of the dead under there ;
But the maggots will burrow right into his bones,
  And the moths at his skull will grow fat,
And in time down will tumble the richly carved
    stones,
  Like the rim of my last summer's hat.

Heaven send me contentment, 'tis all I will ask,
  And great riches I then can despise ;
Make a labor of love of each burdensome task,
  Keep all troublesome clouds from my skies.
I will wish for no more, and I'll sing with delight,
  Till the web of my life shall be spun,
Till the film of death shall shut earth from my
    sight,
  Ere the dawn of eternity's sun.

AN EPISTLE TO A FRIEND.

MR. JAMES CRONLEY.

Old friend, I'm proud to know that fame
Is circling 'round your honor'd name ;
That Fortune from her treasured store,
Has gifts to deal you out galore.
I feel a friend's delight in all
The luck that to your lot may fall.

To ev'ry goal, by honor led,
You travel with determined tread.
No place, however high you'll gain,
But you'll through honest means attain ;
And fill the trust with jealous care,
For those whose wisdom placed you there.
I've known you long, and I revere
Your friendship, which I found sincere.
The years are rolling onward now,
We've silver threads strew'd o'er each brow ;
On life's rough sea we're half way o'er,
And nearing fast the farther shore ;
But, Jim, our bark of life may glide,
Adown Time's steady ebbing tide.
We yet perchance may meet with shocks
From breakers, reefs, and sunken rocks ;
But always at the mast-head high,
True colors you will bravely fly,
And ever keep them there sincere—
You are no changeful privateer—
But like the line-of-battle ship,
Your cable you will freely slip,
To fight till you've the prize in tow,
And never strike a fallen foe.
A trenchant pen you well can wield,
And in the journalistic field
You've nobly won deserv'd applause,

In ev'ry good and worthy cause.
You're climbing to the breezy height
Where I admire you with delight,
Because I know you're tried and true,
And fame can make no change in you.
Oh ! may your star ascendent rise,
Until its brightness dim the eyes
Of those who are with envy green,
Since o'er their heads 'tis plainly seen.
Accept these lines sincerely penn'd
From one whom you have long time kenn'd.
No need to write a sentence more,
I'd but repeat things said before.

"NO SMOKING ON DUTY."

By your leave, my worthy masters,
    I've a word or two to say
Ere I step upon the foot-board,
    On my toilsome trip to-day.
I arise with humble bearing
    To address the powers that be,
Who have caused such tribulation
    To all smokers, such as me.

Long before the beard of manhood
  Blest the scrutinizing stare
Of my many wistful glances
  To detect a coming hair,
I could whiff my granny's dudeen
  With as comical a lip
As a passenger conductor
  When he takes his maiden trip.

Those were years now scarce remembered
  In the dim and misty past,
And since then my smoking habit
  In my nature's anchored fast.
'Twill be difficult to conquer
  Such an appetite I fear.
And before my pipe is mastered
  I will weep in grief sincere.

It has been a loved companion,
  And as cherished as my bride
When the bloom of youth shone on her,
  As she nestled at my side;
And tho' now 'tis black and burned,
  'Tis as cherished as of yore,   .
Like the lov'd one who's still reigning
  In my bosom's inmost core.

In the many revolutions
  We have witnessed on the rail,
It administered consolation
  Which was never known to fail;
And when things were working badly
  On the old mill we bestrode,
It dispelled, in clouds of incense,
  All the troubles of the road.

When the pay car seemed to loiter,
  It grew wheezy, rank and strong;
As if something surely whispered
  That affairs were going wrong.
But when once I'd sign the pay-roll
  'Twas transformed to delight;
Like an old maid's face when beaming
  On the long-sought wedding night.

But messieurs, you are the masters,
  And, of course, you have the brains,
While the nerves old Nature gave us,
  To successful run the trains;
So we yield you strict obedience,
  No infraction shall you find,
From to-day henceforth no smoking
  When on duty—in my mind.

COME, BOYS, FILL YOUR GLASSES.

Come, boys, fill your glasses, and pledge me to-
night,
To the hopes which we sigh for, each long sought
delight.
Let the nectar run freely, the liquid o'erflow,
We will drink to the dregs ere we rise, boys, to go.
Here's success to the standard that's gloriously
seen
On the field where the foemen retreat from the
green!
Where the chains of oppression, which bound us
so long,
Shall be sunder'd by freemen who right every
wrong.

During centuries Slavery's curse on the land,
Kept us bound in her shackles, close tied was each
hand;
In our councils divided, we struggled in vain;
We were conquer'd and beaten again and again;
But the clouds of dissension are drifting away,
And the sun o'er the hill-tops of freedom's fair
day
Is most surely ascending, its beams we can tell;
And our armies are marching with statesman
Parnell.

Our dear forefathers bore every brunt of the
    fray;
And their mail-clad opponents they oft drove
    away;
Many fields can attest what their valor has won,
When each one had a pike, and each foeman a
    gun;
'Gainst the science of war and artillery's roar
They would charge till they'd sink into rivers of
    gore;
Till the plain would be strewed with the dying
    and dead,
And the green flag be floating high over the red!

Now in our day the battle once more is renewed.
We will fight till the last haughty foe is subdued.
All our weapons are modern instruments made;
To be used in the senate, where parties arrayed,
Will be sure to respect us, and hearken to those
Who are flaunting the green in the face of their
    foes;
So, my boys, fill each glass, let us drink with the
    yell
Of our fierce *faugh-a-ballagh for statesman Par-
    nell!

*Clear the way.

THE FIRST GRAY HAIR.

They are coming, boys, they're coming;
   I discovered one to-day;
'Tis a tawny looking stranger,
   And I fear it comes to stay;
On my upper lip, disgusted,
   I espied youth's dreaded foe,
In the spot the ladies lingered,
   When they kissed me long ago !

'Tis a signal on life's railroad,
   Like the caution flags we spy,
When the trackmen fear fast running
   May displace a rail or tie ;
And it tells in tones of warning
   That old Time is jogging on
To the great, unknown hereafter,
   Where earth's multitudes have gone.

'Tis a mystery what brought it ;
   I am not so very old;
Scarcely in the " roaring forties."
   I suppose the heat and cold
Of our slavish occupation,
   At all seasons of the year,
Hurried on the grinning rascal
   That comes prematurely here.

Or perhaps it comes from watching
  Too intently at the gauge,
When the pointer travels backward
  And each moment seems an age,
Trying hard to make a meeting
  With the "flyer," nearly due,
As the water in a torrent
  Courses out of every flue.

There's another cause suspected,
  Which I'll tell in sober sooth :
I was somewhat of an angel
  In the halcyon days of youth !
And I lingered in the temple,
  Where I prayed and fasted long,
Laying treasures up in heaven
  And avoiding doing wrong.

But where'er it came from, surely
  It is here upon my lip,
In the place the sirens dallied
  All those honied joys to sip,
That have ravished soul and senses
  With such keen, ecstatic bliss,
Many twilights spent in rapture,
  Tasting beauty's luscious kiss !

24

Oh, dear Ponce de Leon, tell me,
 From your dwelling in the sky,
Where's the fountain which you sought for?
 Are its waters sealed or dry?
If your search was not rewarded
 When in life you sought its brink,
Now perhaps your clearer vision
 Can direct me where to drink.

I will lave upon its bosom
 Till the wine of life shall course
Through my heart and brain delighted,
 In its glorious, youthful force,
Till all ills and aches shall vanish,
 And the clouds of care roll by,
Till the sun shall shine resplendent
 From a clear, ethereal sky.

I am but a simple rhymer,
 Yet I have a poet's heart,
And, if words would come for calling,
 I'd a lesson here impart
To all coming generations,
 Calling loudly to beware
Of those heart-regrets to haunt them,
 When they spy the first gray hair.

THANKS FOR A CHRISTMAS TURKEY.

To W. B. PHELPS.

DEAR SIR:—My humble thanks I send
To you, my much esteemed, old friend,
Who did my appetite allay,
With turkey roast this Christmas day.
Indeed he was a royal bird,
As e'er amongst his kind was heard
With gobble, strut and chuckle loud,
The king of all the feathered crowd,
His flesh was juicy, tender, sweet,
And brittle, so a babe could eat.
When I beheld him cooked and browned,
With smiling faces seated round
The festive board, I felt the thrill
Of gratitude, carousing still,
      Within my thankful breast ;
With knife and fork I carved him quick,
I severed ev'ry steak as slick
As though a surgeon's scalpel, keen,
Flashed thro' his parts, both fat and lean,
      Then dined with eager zest.

Of all the days throughout the year
To bring us hope, our hearts to cheer,
To-day stands first, for friends unite,
In festive mirth and pure delight.

And when the wassail bowl is full,
The brain must be extremely dull
That will not soar above the ground
To heights where social joy is found.
No monarch, on his throne of state,
Surrounded by the rich and great, .
Could look with hautier disdain
On all the ills in sorrow's train
Than I, when e'er the flowing glass
From friend to friend would freely pass,
  With fellowship of song ;
It can inspire the dullest clod
That ever groveled on the sod,
And make him feel himself a king,
With fancies floating on the wing,
  Through airy heights along.

But here I am, a noted foe
To Bacchus, and the ruddy glow
Of sparkling wine, which bubbles bright,
Around the board on Christmas night.
Yet mem'ries of the olden time
Will float and mingle in my rhyme,
Until I feel a dancing train
Of gleesome fancies in my brain.
Perhaps your king of table fowl
Dispelled Time's sable, monkish cowl,

And let the glow of pleasure glide
Around my heart's quiescent tide,
Until the years rolled with me back
To youth's delightful, festive track,
      And changed me to a boy.
Let moralists, in sober sooth,
Condemn the primrose path of youth ;
I'd rather know I laughed at care
With hearthy, boon companions there,
      Than not have known it's joy.

I'm one amongst the very few
Who've seen the good you slyly do ;
For, like a thief disguised you steal,
Distributing to other's weal.
Your generous heart would fain embrace
Within its bounds the human race ;
You preach a universal creed,
And practice it in word and deed,
·You'll cling to friends through good and ill,
And be their benefactor still.
It matters not where'er the clime
They first stepped on the stage of time,
Or if their skin be black as night,
Or olive, or Caucassian white,
      To you it is the same.
The friendly heart and hand are there,

To deal them out, as free as air,
Remembrances of kindness dear,
And this is why we all revere
      Your noble, honored name.

God bless the good old Christmas time,
I truly pray, in simple rhyme!
And bless the kindness which bestowed
The thoughtful gift on my abode;
And bless the day when tables groan
With plenty, on this changeful zone.
And may the years, with tardy tread,
Pass captivating o'er your head.
And when from hence you're called away,
May Hope's illuminating ray
Assist your footsteps to explore
The pathway to the other shore;
But, sure as are the Scripture's just,
You may go mingle with the dust,
      With heavenly joys in view;
I'll cheerfully submit to Fate,
If in that certain, future state,
I'll pass the dreadful muster roll,
Of Him who'll judge my sinful soul,
      Successfully as you.

FOOT-BOARD REFLECTIONS.

'Mid the sweltering rays of the mid-day sun
  I am here in the cab, while on flying wheels
I must make my long and my tedious run,
  Ere the lengthened ray of the evening steals
Down o'er the track with its cooling shade,
  To soothe the nerves that I oft must strain,
And I sigh as I think of the leafy glade
  Where the rich are bound who are on the train.

Ah, yes, they are off to their cool retreats,
  To their wealthy homes by the sounding sea,
Where their fare consists of the choicest meats,
  With vintage rare as rich wines can be ;
Where Fortune deals from her lavish hand
  The luckiest cards within her pack,
And woos them along with smiling bland,
  Till the autumn breezes drive them back.

What wonder at all if I ponder o'er
  The thousand ills of the luckless poor.
Who must toil 'mid the smoke and ceaseless roar
  Of the daily load which our frames endure ?
And our fare consists of a crust of bread,
  To be moistened oft amid falling tears,
Ere we sink to rest on a thorny bed,
  For a few short hours till the dawn appears.

God pity us all on the road of life,
　　We need His help to prolong the fight
We are forced to make in the daily strife,
　　As we humbly plod on our path of right;
And if by a step we pass its bounds,
　　What a cry is raised by the heartless throng,
Who unleash their pack of bloodthirsty hounds
　　To disjoint our bones for a simple wrong.

A flowery path o'er life's highway, sure,
　　The rich ones find who inherit wealth;
They may glide amid gilded crime secure
　　In the sun's bright ray or in midnight stealth;
But the poor man toils like the veriest slave,
　　At his daily task, in all sorts of weather,
On his lowly road which ends at the grave,
　　To keep his body and soul together.

Sweet hope is unsubstantial food,
　　But for it where would we be to-day?
Discouraging thoughts that dare intrude,
　　Are by its influence driven away.
The crooks and thorns we daily meet
　　Along the route we are forced to tread,
May lead in a year to some cool retreat,
　　Where we'll lie at ease on a downy bed.

YOUR OWN NATIVE TOWN.

From the moment your feet press the earth to
    begin
Your rough march to the grave, in this world's
    great din,
You will find many stumbling blocks thrown in
    your way,
And your armor will often be pierced in the fray.
It will take all your skill to avoid the rude shocks
You will meet on the road against venomous
    rocks,
But the rudest of all you encounter will frown
From the ape-featured crew in your own native
    town.

You may have in your bosom a heart beating true
With ennobling intentions, but they'll misconstrue
Every effort you'll make, as you labor for right,
And they'll poison the air worse than vapors of
    night;
They will fling their insidious stabs at your back,
Just like cowardly assassins, the rancorous pack ;
They will scoff and deride you and kick you when
    down
With unmerciful ire, in your own darling town.

If you'll pause and reflect you will easily note
How those dear ones can tell ev'ry patch on your
    coat ;

Where the meagre purse presses, how bills are
    unpaid;
How your creditors claim you take profit from
    trade;
How your face, though with honesty stamped, is
    a mask;
How your labors of love are a burdensome task;
All the good you've erected will soon be pulled
    down,
By the midge-hearted clan, in your own native
    town.

When you're weighed you're found wanting.
    they'll burden the scales
With foul hints, told suspicious, rank, gossiping
    tales.
Sure they fancy mankind all have hearts like their
    own,
It is thus you are gauged, and your bosom must
    moan.
If you clamber above them, and heed what they
    say,
You will soon be unnerved, and unfit for the fray;
But if brave and determined, by heaven, each
    clown
May assail you in vain in your own darling town!

If you've tact, and ambition, and brains you can
    rise

From their level with ease, and get nearer the
    skies ;
If you've nerve for the battle,a heart for the strife,
You will surely succeed on the highway of life ;
If you've genius, tho' humble, men mention your
    name,
And it gives you a pull at the goblet of fame.
You will float where your filthy detractors will
    drown,
And you'll win some applause in your own native
    town.

Let the buzzards and owls croak in envious mood,
There is joy on the wing as you fly from the brood ;
They are powerless to follow, you laugh at the
    fun ;
Their attacks are like boys throwing stones at the
    sun.
Every man has a mission, fill yours while you
    may,
And if guided by honor, you'll bask in the ray
That will shine in effulgence, and lead to renown,
And defeat of your foes in your own native town.

TO MISS ELLA LEWIS.

A PASSENGER WHO ASSISTED IN RESCUING AN ENGINEER FROM UNDER
HIS WRECKED ENGINE.

Were mine the pen to flash the fire
    Of brilliant thoughts these lines along,
Or wake the grand, heroic lyre,
    In strains of rich, melodious song ;
I'd sing your noble deeds on high,
    Beyond the reach of fleeting fame,
Until my voice would reach the sky,
    To eulogize your laurelled name.

Oh, lady ! 'tis such acts can shine
    And brighten up this vale of tears,
When gentle hands and hearts combine
    To soothe poor suff'ring engineers.
We stand the first to meet the crash ;
    Our duty is to save the train,
And oft with speed of lightning's flash
    We're crushed, dismember'd, scorched or slain.

In silken robes, with jewels bright,
    And both your lovely arms bare,
You stood beside poor, dying Knight,
    And proved a minist'ring angel there.
The fleeting spark of life you fanned,
    Until you felt reviving breath ;

It was your gentle, skillful hand
  That rescued him from painful death.

Ripe, luscious fruit you kindly send,
  The choicest flowers deck his room,
Tho' distant, still you prove his friend,
  And waft around him sweet perfume.
The Shelleys and the Nightingales
  Of lasting fame, you'll stand beside,
Who can assuage the human wails
  They hear upon life's stormy tide.

He's lying now with broken bones,
  And reason gone, within his cot;
Unheard are wife's and children's moans,
  The past, the present, all forgot.
If back to Reason's throne once more
  His mind returns and pauses there,
From out his brave heart's inmost core,
  He'll bless you with a hero's prayer.

If death makes all your efforts vain,
  And ends the life you sought to save,
The engineer of every train
  Who'll stand above his lowly grave
Shall testify in grand acclaim,
  And echo shall prolong the notes,

Till tributes to your honored name
　　Arise from twenty thousand throats!

May life be one continued round
　　Of joyful scenes, 'mid prospects fair,
To you, whose brow is laurel crowned,
　　We cry in earnest, heartfelt prayer.
And when eternal dawn is nigh,
　　As you did here to others do,
May He who rules beyond the sky,
　　Dear lady, do the same to you.

———

NEURALGIA.

Each vein is full of liquid fire,
And every nerve in vengeful ire
Keeps bounding with a keen desire
　　　　To kill me quick;
I cannot get a moment's rest;
My very vitals are distrest;
My patience gets a painful test.
　　　　Oh, Lord, I'm sick!

If every ill the flesh can feel
Combined to make my senses reel,
Neuralgia, you are just the chiel
　　　　To beat them all;

You're thumping me with mighty blows,
You pound me from my head to toes;
The tears now coursing down my nose
      Like rivers fall.

My eyes oft from their sockets start,
My teeth seem pulling all apart,
There is a feeling round my heart
      I can't describe;
My curse upon yourself and kin—
But if at cursing I begin
'Twill last till hell I plunge you in,
      And all your tribe.

TO ALDERMAN BENZ, OSWEGO, N. Y.

My dear Alderman Benz, it surprised me to note,
  How a man of your standing, good judgment
    and tact,
Should be found with your fingers clutched into
    the throat
Of all roads, if the council endorses your act.
'Tis a sleepy old gait for an engine to run,
  And you know in your heart every railroader
    here
Does the best that he can all those mishaps to shun
  That are put to the charge of the poor engineer.

'Twill drive enterprise out of this tax-ridden
    place;
And we haven't a surplus to boast of you, know;
In the summer time grass on our streets you can
    trace,
    And in winter huge hummocks of unsullied
    snow.
Manufacturers never were lured by the bait
    Of "our splendid location for business," be-
    cause
On account of high taxes they will not locate,
    And, besides, they've a dread of our iron-
    bound laws.

When the Welland canal was enlarged we sup-
    posed
    That big fleets from the west at our wharves
    would be seen;
But, alas! from that time until now we reposed
    Undisturbed by increase of our merchant ma-
    rine.
Elevators are sinking to speedy decay,
    Where the rats and the sparrows their timbers
    devour;
Soon the railroads will go just the very same way,
    If you limit our speed down to four miles an
    hour.

Samuel Sloan, with his well equipped roads, has
    done more

For Oswego than all the canals in the land ;
Go with Corporal Phelps down about the lake
    shore,
    Where he'll point to the proof with his figures
      in hand ;
Every month as the paymaster goes on his trip,
    'Tis United States coin which his wallet contains;
It will purchase more flour and potatoes than
    scrip
    For the men who must toil with their sinews
      and brains.

Now reflect on the foregoing facts which I give
    To you here in this paper in shape of a song ;
Let us foster the railroads and help them to live,
    Which they will, if with prudence we help them
      along.
As a city official you've always been found
    On the side where you wielded good sensible
      power ;
Do not mar your past record by girding us 'round
    With a mud turtle movement of four miles an
      hour.

DOUBTS AND TRUTHS.

Off to church I went last Sunday
  In a rather gloomy mood,
I am not a firm believer,
  And I seldom there intrude,
Yet I like to hear a sermon
  Where impassioned words do play
In an eloquent connection,
  Be the subject what it may.
But the speaker, to affect me,
  Must be pious and sincere,
And stand forth a true example
  Of the words which strike my ear;
For I look behind the subject,
  And I closely view the man,
As I'm doing here at present.
  This is how the sermon ran :
"From the mountains and the valleys,
  From the deserts, and each plain,
From the seas, the lakes and oceans,
  There shall march a countless train,
From the birth of time they'll rally
  To the trumpet's clarion call,
As it thunders o'er the world :
  'Come to judgment one and all.'
How the guilty wretch shall totter

In the deepest of dismay!"
It was thus a theologian
  Preached so eloquent that day,
And I thought as he expounded
  Texts of Scripture so devout
He is sure to be an angel
  When the dead shall get the rout,
And to glory everlasting
  He can see his title clear;
If he can, dear sinful reader,
  You and I need never fear.
I have heard of reverend ranters
  Who could point us out the road,
Where the gauge is rather narrow
  Leading to that blest abode.
Ah! how fluently they tell us
  Of the joys beyond the grave
And what sacrifices daily
  We should make, our souls to save;
But when Death would hover near them
  Some physician would be called,
To exert his skill and save them,
  As they'd writhe in fear appalled;
How they dread to go to glory
  That they've preached about for years,
And they die like craven cowards,
  'Tis not so with engineers.

There are hundreds of exceptions
    To that class of hair-brained fools,
Who are pious theologians,
    Who were taught in lib'ral schools;
And they lead their congregations
    Up Mount Pisgahs of the earth,
'Till the glorious Land of Promise
    Dawns in full, celestial birth!
To no sect nor creed they're wedded,
    To no dogmas bound in chains;
But upon broad Christian tenets
    They employ prolific brains;
I respect them, they are sages,
    And I'll follow where they tread;
All my caustic written notions
    Have been pointed at each head
Of the hypocritic swaddlers,
    Who enjoy this life below,
And keep preaching of the future
    Where they ne'er expect to go.
If to live in full and plenty,
    And to sleep on beds of down,
Is the trunk-line up to Heaven
    They are sure of glory's crown.
If to toil with brain and sinew
    'Till the heart-strings nearly crack,
Running daily on an engine,

Over old and worn-out track ;
When the driving-springs are flattened,
  And the pistons blowing strong,
And the flues are leaking badly,·
  And the valves are beating wrong,
And the pumps are out of order,
  And the boxes full of smoke,
And the rods all thumping loudly,
  Every time she makes a stroke—
If such things torment us daily
  While on earth in grief we dwell,
I have hopes, dear, patient reader,
  That we'll not be switched for hell.

In the foremost ranks of danger,
  We are daily forced to tread ;
And our firemen stand beside us,
  As we battle for our bread ;
We ne'er shirk the post of duty,
  Altho' Death keeps closely by,
For, full conscious of our peril,
  We can resolutely die.
I disclaim all idle boasting
  We have heros in the tomb,
Whom the public know were martyrs,
  Ere their youth had lost its bloom.
Show me 'mongst the ranks of labor

Such a roll-call of the brave,
  As the engineers and firemen
Who sleep in the hero's grave!

Hark! I hear the "caller" coming
  And the crimson streaks of day,
Shooting up athwart the heavens,
  Tell 'tis time to go away.

———

TO THE REV. F. H. BECK.

WRITTEN AFTER READING HIS POEM ON THE "BOOK AGENT."

Reverend Sir:

'Twill surprise you these lines to peruse,

Which I wrote after reading the song of your
  Muse.

What a tormenting time the book agent should
  come,

As you studied your sermon alone in your room.

Oh! I thought: were I there in that clergyman's
  place

I would hammer some texts on the book agent's
  face,

Which the public could read for the good of man-
  kind

From the "Last Publication," more fierce than
  refined.

Take the man who has patience sufficient to hear
A glib canvasser's tongue, as it wags at his ear.
He may truly lay claim to salvation and say,
"Sure the Lord in His mercy has tried me to-day ;
For He sent me a tempter like Satan of yore,
In the guise of a man with a plentiful store
Of persuasion, and I kept my patience secure
'Till "I bowed out" the tempter away from my
    door."

Well, the "he-ones" are bad when they come
    with their books,
But the "she-devil's" worse with her man-kill-
    ing looks,
With her smirks and her smiles, and her artful
    complaints ;
And a tale made to draw forth compassion from
    saints,
With her wiles stealing 'round, sweet as May-
    morning dew,
Or those spice gales that blow in the vales of
    Peru ;
It is then you require a "John Sullivan" blow
That shall drive her away with a thundering
    "No!"

There are many things "tucked by translators"
    in creeds,
But the man who can list to a book agent's needs

For an hour, and not kick him out into the street,
Is a canonized saint from his head to his feet;
Oh, I hope you are such, and I love to peruse
Every flash from the pen of your eloquent Muse.
And I hope you will not deem my freedom a
    crime,
When I greet you, dear sir, as a brother in rhyme.

A SONG FOR THE BOYS.

I'm afflicted with ills of the flesh, boys,
    And I'll share my misfortune with you;
They are stripes from humanity's lash, boys,
    Only shunned by the virtuous few.
Saints are scarce on the railroad to-day, boys,
    From the president down to the chap
Who is flagging for very poor pay, boys,
    With his hair sticking out through his cap.

I've a rheumatic twinge in my toes, boys,
    And a kink in the small of my back;
They are sure to disturb my repose, boys,
    When in bed or when out on the track.
I have feasted on quail and on toast, boys,
    From my grub-bucket daily for years;
Sure I don't know of men who can boast, boys,
    Of such feeding unless engineers.

Our conductors have napkins and rings, boys,
  Silver knives, forks and spoons, and choice
    plate;
Sure we scoff at such fanciful things, boys,
  As we dine on our engines in state.
With our fingers and thumbs we can throw, boys,
  A square meal down our throats pretty quick,
It was thus Adam feasted, you know, boys,
  Before Eve made a "mash" on old Nick.

Of high living I'd have you keep clear, boys,
  It is loaded with numerous ills ;
And besides, shun the schooner of beer, boys,
  Yes, and worm-juice flowing through stills.
They are stumbling blocks spread for your feet,
    boys,
  Like the smiles of a widow through tears,
Every one of them full of deceit, boys,
  And a trap to catch poor engineers.

I intended a moral to write, boys,
  'Till the widows ran into my head,
So I think I'll set brakes for to-night, boys,
  And retire to my virtuous bed.
Ere the morrow's bright sun shall arise, boys,
  I must up and have at it again,
For, no matter how stormy the skies, boys,
  I'll be called to depart with my train.

WRITTEN UNDER A PHOTOGRAPHIC GROUP.

Ye Gods ! behold this handsome crowd
So self-conceited, vain and proud,
Who pose before the artist's eye
Beneath a gray, October sky !
They're frizzed, and combed, in Sunday style,
While some men frown and others smile.
But Nagle's photographic art
Shall beauty to each face impart.

He tries to get them in repose,
He twists each chin, surveys each nose,
Until he has the " awkward squad "
All grouped upon the verdant sod.
And, now, as each one looks so grand,
When polished by some barber's hand,
I'll take a pencil picture, too,
Of ev'ry face I see in view.

See Rowan, on the left who sits,
To flank the crowd of sports and wits,
And at his side I plainly trace
The handsome phiz of Patrick Grace.
See honest Paddy sitting there
With grizzled beard and unkempt hair.
The next is P. F. Johnson's form,
Whom all admire with feelings warm.

Bob Gettings, from the barber's hand,
Looks sleek, and smooth, with features bland,
And at his side the piercing eye
Of Dennis Connelly I spy.
"Judge" Glynn behold, he sits at ease,
The artist's glance he's sure to please.
See Crawford, self-possessed and proud,
The valiant "jumbo" of the crowd.

Sweet William Grant your head hold down,
Do not on old companions frown.
Brave Gill, who never missed a fight
In Union wars, is on your right.
Note Tim McCarthy in life's prime
Near Fennell, author of this rhyme.
See Dorsey, too, the ladies' joy,
A good, straight-forward, handsome boy.

Behold Omelia standing there,
Behind Commiss'ner Grace's chair.
See Hanley from the Second ward
Whose head with good sound sense is stored.
There's Chris, an angel in disguise,
Whose look expresses pain'd surprise.
Jack Sculley's last, he bears his weight
On Grant, which makes him stand so straight.

Well, here we are, and seventeen
More jovial lads were seldom seen;
All cast in Nature's stalwart mold,
And prized for strength far more than gold.
Upon the rugged road of life
We win our bread, 'mid toil and strife,
And thankful all for robust health,
Which is our only source of wealth.

Perhaps my boys, in after years,
When Time shall change our smiles to tears,
When we'll be wrinkled, old and gray,
These pictures shall recall the day
We met, in manhood's strength and pride,
With joke and jest, on ev'ry side,
To let the artist group us all,
Outside Oswego's City Hall.

SOME TRUTH IN RHYME.

While perusing the papers last evening, I read
Of a deeply laid plan to deprive men of bread;
'Tis ingenious indeed, I must freely confess,
And may make by perversion a deal of distress
'Mongst the ranks of the toilers all over the land;
If their tongues run unguarded, their doom is at
    hand.

I supposed that by blacklisting those who rebel,
Was a torture on earth to prepare men for hell.

More refined in their cruelty daily they grow;
With their scorpion whips they afflict men with
    woe,
In the shape of detectives to follow them round,
So their masters may know where disturbers are
    found.
In the lodge room they'll mingle and talk with
    the boys,
And by oily persuasion enlarge on those joys
To be had for the seeking, beyond their desires;
Then betray them like erstwhile the Mollie
    Maguires.

If such tactics increase with the growth of the
    years,
Sure the Lord only knows what we poor engineers
Must all do for a living; I fear we will starve,
If a plan can't be found airy nothings to carve!
And a dish of wind-pudding contrived from our
    breath,
To protect us from hunger and save us from
    death.
Oh! if such is discovered we'll chorus in glee
Without fear of starvation, for water is free!

Listen, boys ; I've an antidote here for your ills,
You will find it far safer than powder or pills :
Keep your tongues in your cheeks, do not dare let
    them wag ;
Should that fail, in each mouth stuff a close-fitting
    gag ;
If you do, you'll have nothing to fear boys, because
There's no danger at all from our rules or our
    laws,
Unless grossly perverted by those who'd destroy
The best organization in railroad employ.

We shall always be faithful to men whom we
    serve,
From the strict line of duty we never shall swerve,
We are true to their interests, give them our lives,
Never thinking of dear ones, our children and
    wives.
When the martyrs to duty are called from the
    grave,
Engineers will be first in the ranks of the brave,
With their firemen beside them they'll march to
    the fore,
Where eternal reward will be theirs evermore.

THREE TOASTS.

Come, my boys, the decanter fill full till we drink
A few toasts here to-night, let our hearts never
  sink,
For in wine there is pleasure, let lunatics bawl
About poison therein, to the de'il with them all.
Every man fill his glass till the beads bubble o'er,
We will drink it to-night, and we drank it before.
Get you ready, clasps hands with a hearty hurrah.
Now the toast! " Here's success to you Erin-go-
  Bragh!"

They are drained! Let us fill them to flowing
  again,
Till we pledge in full bumpers the brave-hearted
  men
Who defy every dungeon, the scaffold, and block,
And can fight for her freedom, with hearts like
  the rock.
Who are trying to burst every link of the chain
That is binding her limbs and is causing her pain.
Now the toast! drink it standing, the chorus shall
  swell
Here's to all who are with you, dear leader, Par-
  nell!

Fill once more while we're sober, although 'tis
  the last
Till again we assemble to talk of the past;

And to plan for the future, as true men should do,
Who've a country to wrench from a despotic
crew.
See ! the sun is just rising far off in the east,
He will soon shed his beams on our wine-drinking
feast ;
Now, my boys, stand in order, drink freely to those
Who will never give up till we conquer our foes.

DUTY'S CALL.

RAILROADING ON THE B. U. L.

"Wake up from sleep" the caller said,
I quickly bounded out of bed,
A stupid feeling in my head,
        When roused in such a fury ;
I thought I scarcely closed my eyes,
He routed me in such surprise.
I'll curse him till the day he dies,
        In spite of judge or jury.

Three hundred miles my aching back
Was bounded o'er uneven track ;
My stiffened joints were fit to crack,
        From such a constant motion.
I suffered more than tongue can tell,

Far worse than imps confined in—well
We rolled about in every swell,
  Like ships upon the ocean.

My brothers, in a sunny clime,
Who read this simple, truthful rhyme,
You little know the awful time
  We have in frosty weather;
We blow our fingers and our thumbs
To keep them warm, we dine on crumbs,
Or grub dished up in boarding slums,
  Where dozens hive together.

In drifts of snow we nearly freeze,
Exposed to ev'ry cutting breeze;
The glass tells twenty-five degrees
  Below what men call "zero."
Our noses have a hazy hue—
A most repulsive looking blue—
Besides, our whole official crew,
  Have hearts as hard as Nero.

They drive us out when needing sleep,
A harvest for themselves to reap;
Because they get our labor cheap,
  And pay in scrip quite often.
The rails are only half way tied,

26

The joints apart are opened wide,
'Tis certain death for men to ride
    When Spring embankments soften.

My heart would bound with honest joy,
If I could find some good employ,
Where callers never would annoy
    A man from night till morning;
And where no snow-drifts would be seen,
Where fields would wear perennial green,
And skies would always look serene,
    Our lives in joy adorning.

Perhaps good luck I yet may meet,
And get away from snow and sleet,
To some choice clime where tranquil heat
    To railroad men is given;
The only place I'm sure to find
A climate, suited to my mind,
Where evermore I'll feel resigned,
    Is up with God in Heaven.

TO KITTIE BLAINE.

Miss(?) Kittie Blaine—perhaps the "Miss"
   Is not the proper thing to write,
Yet, in a dream of perfect bliss,
   I'll fancy you a maid to-night—
Your lines upon the engineer
Are truthful, musical, sincere,
And I, an humble rhyming chap,
Now doff to you my greasy cap,
In heartfelt thanks for such a song
As you so kindly sent along,
To cheer us up, and drive despair
Away from hearts consumed by care.
We've all been cooped in cabs for years,
Like hens, when house-wives have their fears
That neighbor's stones may thin the brood
Of scratching thieves, when seeking food.
In summer, winter, spring and fall,
We must respond to duty's call.
We're blanched and beaten by the blast,
Our blooming cheeks are fading fast,
We're friendless, save yourself, I find
Your sex are silent or unkind;
They never send a word along
To cheer us up, much less a song.
But now we will enthrone you queen

Of all the boys throughout the land.
Where e'er a smoky phiz is seen
  A heart is there at your command.

If my rheumatic harp could sing
  Such music as your gifted lyre,
I'd make the hills and valleys ring
  Our thanks in true, poetic fire.
In numbers we're an army now,
With hero stamped on every brow.
For you have proved it in your song,
And, madam, you have told no wrong;
Indeed we know you were sincere
When writing on the engineer.
Suppose we enter partnership,
And cruise upon a rhyming trip;
I'll pass the work rough-hewn to you,
Your dainty fingers soon can do
The pruning, trimming, weeding out,
Of vulgar words I strew about;
I'll tell you of our daily joys—
The pleasures surfeiting the boys—
The grandeur of the scenes we pass,
Until they seem a moving mass,
Parading for our special sight,
On cloudless day and fogless night.
Then you can weave a song-boquet,

And sing it to the brothers all;
While I can bask in beauty's ray,
  A willing slave who loves the thrall!

Please give me your attention now,
  Sweet songstress! and don't think me rude,
Nor cloud your genius-crested brow,
  If I offensively intrude
By making some inquiries, so
I'll ascertain how far to go
In my expressions as I rhyme
The thanks of men you've sung sublime.
Now, tell—oh, dear! I'm so afraid—
Please mention if you are a maid?
If so, by mighty Jove! I swear,
You're launched on life with prospects fair,
And soon shall find a dear one, true,
Who'll more than brother be to you;
Who'll press on your melodious lips
Delights that other joys eclipse.
Perhaps you are a faithful wife,
And coupled up to one for life,
Who, like myself, toils ev'ry day
For pleasure, disregarding pay;
If so you are a happy spouse,
And mistress of some cozy house.
If you a blooming widow be—

My stars! How impudent of me,
To sneak Paul Prying, but, if so,
I do respect your weeds and woe!
For widows who've been sore distrest
I have a soft spot 'neath my vest!
Some dear departed boys I've laid
Beneath the sod, and often prayed
With all their poor heart-broken wives,
For God to guard their lonely lives.
Some other chaps have done the same,
Successful too! and " blocked my game!"
But be you widow, wife, or maid,
In blooming youth, or near the shade
Of ripened years, where art must hide
The buffets met on life's rough tide,
I thank you truly and 1 know
    My brothers of the foot-board here,
Express the same, with hearts aglow,
    For praising up the engineer.

SABBATH MUSINGS.

There's a rhyming fit upon me, and its prompt-
        ings I obey,
In a crude, unmeasured jingle, on this holy Sab-
        bath day,
As the bells for church are chiming, and I'll note
        some passers by

And describe them in my stanzas, as familiar ones
    I spy.

Here comes Eggleston in meekness, with a hymn
    book in his hand,
And beside him strides an angel by the name of
    L. O. Rand ;
They're a pious pair of play-boys as e'er punched
    a duplex true,
Dressed in Sunday-go-to-meetings, for a snooze
    within the pew.

Dan is something of an angler, he can " whip a
    stream " in style,
He entices fish from water with a sanctimonious
    smile.
In a piscatorial manner he enlarges on his luck,
And regrets the loss of monsters that escape from
    off his hook.

Rand is quite a different fellow, one who never
    tells a lie,
But keeps plodding upward surely to a mansion
    in the sky,
Charlie Fisk says Rand will get there if St. Peter's
    at the door,
When he hears him tell a story, he will punch his
    ticket sure.

Well, my own opinion, truly, of this trio—it is
    this:

If they ever enter heaven to reside in homes of
    bliss

They'll deceive the Chief Conductor, all who know
    them will agree,

And, besides, dear sinful reader, there's a chance
    for you and me.

But the bells have ceased their tolling. I must
    hie me with the throng,

I regret to close abruptly this discordant, truth-
    ful song,

Yet, upon some near occasion I will make a little
    noise,

Telling all the Monthly's readers what I know
    about the boys.

———

THE WINTER WINDS WHISTLE.

The winter winds whistle,
    The skies frown in wrath,
Misfortune seems driving
    On merciless path.

The snowdrifts are piling
    On mountain and moor,
A sight which is dreadful
    To those who are poor.

There's joy for the wealthy,
  Whose clothing is warm
When Boreas is reigning,
  The king of the storm.

But we who are fighting
  For bread which we eat,
Must suffer fresh torments
  And luckless defeat.

Each day brings its sorrow,
  And night brings no rest,
Nor hope for the morrow,
  When thus we're oppressed.

Yet, Hope is a siren,
  She woos us along
With coaxing delusive,
  And false, fickle song.

Obscured is the future,
  'Tis dark to our view,
But onward we're driven
  The path to pursue.

Perhaps the bright portals
  Of fortune shall ope—
Ah ! down you deluder,
  That wish sprung from hope.

"COPY."

Dear reader, perhaps you have threaded
    The verge of old Satan's domain;
Or may be at times you've been wedded,
    To imps which have marched in his train,
Or suffered in torture and trouble,
    When bumpers of grief bubbled o'er,
If so, all your ills were a bubble,
    Compared with my sorrowful store.

I am now "in the hands of my printer,"
    And "copy" he cries, with a growl
Which sounds like old Boreas in winter,
    When forth full of vengeance he'll howl.
'Tis "copy" both night, noon, and morning,
    The rascal repeatedly dins;
I'd torture the wretch without warning,
    If he were absolved from his sins.

If dull and insipid I'm feeling,
    No mercy he shows me at all;
But all of my senses go reeling
    When lustily for "copy" he'll bawl.
I scream in the direst distraction,
    And wander to places alone,
Where, free from his prying detection,
    In anguish I ruefully moan.

When whips are cracked tirelessly o'er us,
    The brain will scarce ever reply ;
'Tis seldom we sing in free chorus,
    When made by such means to comply ;
But if we've no fear of a master,
    The Muse will delight on the wing,
And " copy " will surely flow faster,
    When thus full of freedom we sing.

CONTENTS.

www.ingramcontent.com/pod-product-compliance
Lightning Source LLC
Chambersburg PA
CBHW030813110726
47900CB00006B/1612